POETRY OF THE TALIBAN

POETRY
of the
TALIBAN

Translated by
Mirwais Rahmany
&
Hamid Stanikzai

Edited and introduced by
Alex Strick van Linschoten
&
Felix Kuehn

Preface by
Faisal Devji

HURST & COMPANY, LONDON

For S.

First published in the United Kingdom in 2012 by
C. Hurst & Co. (Publishers) Ltd.,
41 Great Russell Street, London, WC1B 3PL

Printed in India

A Cataloguing-in-Publication data record for this book
is available from the British Library.

ISBNs:
978-184904-111-9 *clothbound*
978-184904-305-2 *paperback*

www.hurstpublishers.com

PUBLISHER'S NOTE
The Editors and Publishers have made every effort to identify
the authors of the poems published in this collection. If we have
incorrectly attributed authorship of any of the poems we shall be
pleased to correct the error in our next printing of the volume.

Contents

Mirwais Rahmany was born in Rodat district of Nangarhar province in 1983. He learnt English from his father at an early age. Rahmany fled to Pakistan in the late 1980s on account of the Soviet invasion. He returned to Kabul following the *mujahedeen* victory, but settled in Herat after the civil war broke out among various jihadi groups. In 2001 he began his medical studies at Herat University, from which he graduated in 2008. During this time he also worked as an English teacher in Herat. Most recently, he has done work as a specialised legal translator. He continues to live in Herat.

Abdul Hamid Stanikzai was born in Deh Bali, Kapisa province. He lived there for three years before moving to Kunduz province. Eventually, his parents moved permanently to Kabul. He started school in 1979, and by 1989 enrolled in Kabul's Police Academy. He started his first official job as a computer operator in the Cartography Head Office in 2001. Following that he began translating and writing and is currently studying for a BBA at the Dunya Institute of Higher Education and French at the Lycée Esteqlal in Kabul. He has translated a wide variety of documents, from project manuals, electoral laws and procedures, codes of conduct and so forth, between English, Pashto and Dari.

ABOUT THE EDITORS

A graduate of the School of Oriental and African Studies (BA Arabic and Persian), *Alex Strick van Linschoten* first came to Afghanistan six years ago as a tourist. In 2006, together with Felix Kuehn he founded AfghanWire, an online research and media-monitoring group to give a more prominent voice to local Afghan media. During this time he worked on a translation of the last book of poems published by Nadia Anjuman before her death, *Smoke-veined Flower*. In spring 2010 he published *My Life With the Taliban*, of which he was a co-editor, to critical acclaim. In early 2012 he published *An Enemy We Created*, a history of the relationship between the Afghan Taliban and al-Qaeda, together with Felix Kuehn. He is currently working on a book and PhD at the War Studies Department of Kings College London on the identity of the Afghan Taliban movement 1978–2001. He has worked as a freelance journalist in Afghanistan, Syria, Lebanon and Somalia, writing for *Foreign Policy, International Affairs, ABC Nyheter, The Sunday Times, Globe and Mail* and *The Tablet*. He speaks Arabic, Farsi, Pashtu and German and can get by in French and Dutch.

Felix Kuehn first travelled to Afghanistan some five years ago, having spent several years in the Middle East including a short twelve months in Yemen, where he first learnt Arabic in 2002. In 2006, together with Alex Strick van Linschoten he founded AfghanWire, an online research and media-monitoring group to give a more prominent voice to local Afghan media. In spring 2010 he published *My Life With the Taliban*, for which he was a co-editor, to critical acclaim. In early 2012 he published *An Enemy We Created*, a history of the relationship between the Afghan Taliban and al-Qaeda, together with Alex Strick van Linschoten. Felix holds a degree from the School of Oriental and African Studies (BA Arabic and Development Studies).

ABOUT FAISAL DEVJI

Faisal Devji is University Reader in Modern South Asian History at St Antony's College, University of Oxford. He has held faculty positions at the New School in New York, Yale University and the University of Chicago, from where he also received his PhD in Intellectual History. Devji was Junior Fellow at the Society of Fellows, Harvard University, and Head of Graduate Studies at the Institute of Ismaili Studies in London, from where he directed post-graduate courses in the Near East and Central Asia. He sits on the editorial board of the journal *Public Culture*. Devji is the author of three books, *Landscapes of the Jihad: Militancy, Morality, Modernity* (Hurst, 2005), *The Terrorist in Search of Humanity: Militant Islam and Global Politics* (Hurst, 2009) and *The Impossible Indian: Gandhi and the Temptation of Violence* (Hurst, 2012) and is currently writing a book on the emergence of Muslim politics and the founding of Pakistan. He is interested in the political thought of modern Islam as well as in the transformation of liberal categories and democratic practice in South Asia. Devji's broader concerns are with ethics and violence in a globalised world, particularly with the thought and practices of Mahatma Gandhi, who was among the earliest and perhaps the most perceptive commentator on this predicament of our times.

ACKNOWLEDGEMENTS

This book began its life as a hobby and, as such, we tinkered with the poems for several years before considering whether to compile them for publication. In doing so we were fortunate enough to make the acquaintance of many Afghans and non-Afghans who deepened our understanding of the Taliban movement and Afghanistan itself.

At the top of this list are friends in and from *loy* Kandahar. The sensitivity of this project means it is inadvisable to list names. We hope you know who you are, and that we would not be able to do our work in southern Afghanistan without you.

Most poems were initially translated for the AfghanWire website and media-monitoring service. We were assisted by four excellent translators at that time, and we thank them for their hard work. At a later stage, M. M. helped gather most of the pre-2001 poems for us; this included large numbers of transcriptions from tapes, and we thank him for his work.

We had useful conversations around the edges of this project with various specialists, all of whom helped us in various ways: Orzala Ashraf, Erin Cunningham, Huma Imtiaz, Tom Johnson, Daniel Kimmage, Thomas Hegghammer, Joanna Nathan, Michael Semple, Joshua White and Aaron Zelin.

Staff at Hurst were always welcoming and helpful. Thanks to Jon de Peyer, Daisy Leitch, Rob Pinney and Radha Spratt. Thanks, also, to Fatima Jamadar for yet another perfectly-pitched book cover.

Robert Caron went above and beyond in offering comments, suggestions and interventions that helped improve the final manuscript. The final product is much better for his sage advice.

Many thanks to both Faisal Devji and Michael Dwyer for discussions about the poems themselves, the format of the book, and the substance of introductory pages. Both were extremely patient with the very late delivery of this manuscript.

Alex Strick van Linschoten adds: I would also like to take the opportunity to thank some of my schoolteachers from some years back, without whom I most likely would never have worked on a book like this. All taught me the value of close-reading and the appreciation that – in art – there is more to life than the purely political. Thank you Lucy Beckett, David Bowman, Andrew Carter, Narguess Farzad, Rachel Fletcher and Bill Leary.

Preface

Faisal Devji

At your Christmas, Bagram is alit and bright;
On my *Eid*, even the rays of the sun are dead.
Suddenly at midnight, your bombs bring the light;
In our houses, even the oil lamps are turned off.

Khepulwaak, *On Eid*

The contrast drawn in the lines above between Americans celebrating Christmas in the Bagram Air Base and Afghans commemorating the Muslim festival of Eid outside is so simple as to be unanswerable. However slanted it might otherwise be, this brief description represents a truth beyond the politics of good intentions that characterises the international community's actions in Afghanistan. Ultimately it is likely to be such descriptions that come to define the war in that country, and not the complicated arguments of those who would rescue it from the depredations of Al-Qaeda or the Taliban. Now that coalition forces are preparing to withdraw from Afghanistan without achieving any of their goals, such arguments are about to fall silent in any case, and a new society will have to be built from the kind of consciousness that is on display in this and other poems that may be said to constitute the literature of the Taliban.

It is no exaggeration to say that in the ever-increasing archive of studies on the Taliban only a minuscule number have attended to the movement's aesthetic dimension, including the work of James Caron and Michael Semple. For whether scholars and indeed experts of all kinds view them as being products either of some Western modernity, in the form of the US-backed *jihad* against the Soviets, for example, or on the contrary of an Islamic tradition, the Taliban are invariably defined in terms of tribal regulation and religious law. But however important such juridical and political factors have been in the making of their movement, surely it is the human element, represented in what turns out to be a prolific culture of versification, that goes some way towards accounting for the Taliban's self-consciousness, to say nothing about their resilience and appeal. For this body of verse is part of a greater world of poetic production in which Afghans belonging to every shade of political opinion participate.

Even when the large store of poetry produced by the Taliban or their supporters has been noticed, which is more often than not by American military analysts, it tends to be seen merely as propaganda and thus folded back into the instrumentality of politics. Yet it might well be the autonomy of this aesthetic, or rather its general and broadly human character, that links the Taliban to a wider world outside their ethnic and doctrinal limits. And such a link, of course, is as capable of diluting the movement's integrity as of reinforcing it. So apart from engaging with a subject that has received scant attention until now, this book is remarkable for attending to the expansive and therefore richly ambiguous nature of Taliban verse. And this is hardly surprising given the linguistic and historical situation of the Pashto language, which has for centuries now been in a state of constant engagement with the literary traditions of languages like Persian and Urdu that link the Pashtuns to Iran on the one hand and India on the other.

Now the Taliban are known not only in the West, but in much of the Muslim world, too, for their strict conservatism rather than for any delicate feelings of humanity, yet the poetry associated with them is replete with such fine emotions. Drawing upon the long tradition of Persian or Urdu verse as much as Afghan legend and recent history, it is an aesthetic form that includes unrequited love, powerful women for whose illicit favours competitors vie, and descriptions of natural beauty among its themes, as the following quatrains from a poetess with the pen name Nasrat (Victory) illustrate:

My competitor cut my heart;
Tears streamed from my eyes.
O relentless one, your heart is harder than stone;
I weep for you and you laugh at me.

We love these dusty and muddy houses;
We love the dusty deserts of this country.
But the enemy has stolen their light;
We love these wounded black mountains.

Indeed a common claim in this poetry is that the simple humanity of rural Afghans, nourished by the loveliness of their mountains, meadows and streams, is under attack by coalition forces with their drones, air strikes and heavily armed soldiers. This is of course a literary trope, whose distance from reality does not, however, mean that Taliban poets and their audiences have no genuine feeling for such things as natural beauty. Indeed the contrary is probably true, with the Taliban's aesthetic doing as much to heighten an Afghan's appreciation of flowers, birds and the landscape as of turning him against American troops. But the concern in this literature for humanity is more complex, with some writers sorrowfully acknowledging its loss among the Afghans themselves, as in the following lines from a poem by Samiullah Khalid Sahak entitled *Humanity*:

> Everything has gone from the world,
> The world has become empty again.
> Human animal.
> Humanity animality.
> Everything has gone from the world,
> I don't see anything now.
> All that I see is
> My imagination.
>
> They don't accept us as humans,
> They don't accept us as animals either.
> And, as they would say,
> Humans have two dimensions.
> Humanity and animality,
> We are out of both of them today.
>
> We are not animals,
> I say this with certainty.
> But,
> Humanity has been forgotten by us,
> And I don't know when it will come back.
> May *Allah* give it to us,
> And decorate us with this jewellery.
> The jewellery of humanity,
> For now it's only in our imagination.

If their pastoral idyll strikes us as being so familiar as to be almost universal, the same holds true for the Taliban's aesthetic more generally, which eschews any of the factors that otherwise distinguish the movement, whether it be religious restrictions, sanguinary punishment or the suppression of women. Neither Mullah Mohammad Omar, moreover, nor the regime he led in Afghanistan before 9/11, receives much mention in this poetic cornucopia, though there are references to a longed-for revolution and the establishment of an Islamic moral order. But why should the Taliban's aesthetic be so removed from the opinions and practices that define them both religiously and politically? To account for such a division by invoking ideas about hypocrisy or propaganda is unsatisfactory, because their very possibility would have made Taliban verse controversial and perhaps even impossible. Instead of which it both draws upon and finds acceptance within a poetic tradition that links the movement to a world outside its own. The Taliban's aesthetic, as I have already suggested, is marked by a consciousness external to their movement, one that moves beyond the limits of ideology to make for a thoroughly individual sense of freedom which can manifest itself in obedience as much as defiance, fidelity to a cause as much as its betrayal.

INSIDE, OUTSIDE AND IN BETWEEN

From its origins in the Soviet invasion of 1979, the war that continues to wreck Afghanistan has also given rise to an extraordinary aesthetic consciousness. By weaving it into carpets, photographing it in secret studios and commemorating it in song and verse distributed by way of CDs and cell phones, Afghans across the political spectrum have struggled to humanise a long and destructive war in an effort that bears comparison to the cultural productivity of the First World War in Europe. Poetry, which was probably the most important aesthetic medium of traditional Afghan society, has played a crucial role in this effort, and the Taliban verse collected in this volume represents the melancholy beauty of the old lyric as well as the moral outrage and call to action that is characteristic of modern literature. Unlike the unabashed propaganda that characterises the official audio CDs and other products of the Cultural Committee of the Islamic Emirate, this material by individual members or sympathisers of the Taliban is not only more spontaneous in nature, but also serves to link the movement with a much larger world of aesthetic experience and literary reference outside.

While it is the *tarana* or ballad that seems to be the favourite genre of the Cultural Committee's propaganda, a primarily oral form of literature that has also received most attention from those who study the Taliban, it appears to be the *ghazal* or love lyric whose themes if not always form dominate the movement's unofficial literature. Made up of interlinked couplets that do not have to possess any continuity of narrative or even mood, the *ghazal* is by far the most popular genre of poetry in the region, which can be sung and recited, but also dominates the written literature that was previously composed primarily by court poets and mystics. Indeed the traditional element in the Taliban's aesthetic derives precisely from mystical and courtly or profane works that might not otherwise meet with the movement's approval. Ambiguity lies at the heart of this lyrical tradition, in which emotions, ideas and worlds of reference can change radically from one couplet to another in the same poem, and whose stock characters include despondent lovers, cruel and beautiful mistresses, and a great deal of wine. And it is because such lovers may also be identified with seekers after divine union or courtiers pledged to their prince; such mistresses with God, kings or even beautiful young men; and such wine with spiritual as much as material intoxication, that this poetic tradition is so ambiguous. Indeed the rules of the genre require the *ghazal* to be read at as many different levels as possible. The combination of such levels is clear in the following couplets from a *ghazal* called "Injured" by a poet with the pen name Khairkhwa (Well-wisher):

> I stoned him with the stones of light tears
> Then I hung my sorrow on the gallows like Mansour.

> Like those who have been killed by the infidels,
> I counted my heart as one of the martyrs.

> It might have been the wine of your memory
> That made my heart drunk five times.

While the lyric's ambiguity may have allowed it to escape the strictures of the devout in the past, it also permitted the profane imagery of wine, women and song to be inserted into the language of devotion itself. But to describe this as a repressed or vicarious enjoyment of immoral practices is to miss the point, since what I think is most important about this situation is the establishment of freedom as an internal quality. The limitations of the external world, in other words, are matched by the creation of a liberated consciousness, one that can uphold the moral order while at the same time being detached from it. Rather than separating the profane world from the sacred, then, the aesthetic tradition of which the Taliban's poetry is a part joins them together while dividing the individual's consciousness. Looking at the moral order from outside its own demesne, the individual presupposed by this aesthetic can both uphold and escape it, which also means that he cannot be confined within the precincts of any ideology.

The divided consciousness of this aesthetic subject has in the past been described almost exclusively in terms of mysticism, with the outer world's prohibited pleasures coming to represent the moral order's inner truth. So Islam's masculine God can in this literary tradition be portrayed as a woman of easy virtue, and a figure like Mansour al-Hallaj, who was executed for heresy in medieval Baghdad, praised as a martyr to love. Such a mystical interpretation of the lyric's aesthetic is, for instance, perfectly appropriate where the poetry of a Shia thinker like the Ayatollah Khomeini is concerned. But given the Taliban's professed distaste of such an overtly esoteric approach, their use of its aesthetic suggests that it has become an autonomous and highly flexible mode of consciousness, one that is capable of transforming all outward forms into their opposites in the realm of inner pleasures. Thus the veil that is officially described as a garment representing women's modesty and virtue comes in this poetic tradition to stand for coquetry and sexual desire. This is how the inner value of all things is determined by the converse of their outer meaning.

Of course the Taliban were not the first to dissociate the double consciousness of traditional aesthetics from the practice of mysticism. That privilege belongs to the nationalists and Marxists of the twentieth century, who would often identify the lyric's beloved with the state or revolution they longed to lead. But deployed by these secular ideologies, the *ghazal*'s themes tended to lose their transgressive appeal and become bland symbols. And though the Taliban's religious character saves their poetry from such impoverishment, it is no less modern than the literature of the communists and nationalists. For it is probably from these latter groups that the non-traditional elements of the Taliban's aesthetic derive, including as they do rousing calls to action and astute analyses of

16

industrial society that give the lie to any notion of the movement's folkish character. Here, for example, are some lines from a poem called "London Life", by Sa'eed:

There are clouds and rain but it doesn't have any character;
Life has little joy or happiness here.
Its bazaars and shops are full of goods,
These kinds of goods don't have a value.
Life here is so much lost in individuals that,
Brother to brother and father to son, there is no affection.

Their knowledge is so great that they drill for oil in the depths of the oceans,
But even this knowledge doesn't give them a good reputation.
I see their many faults and virtues with my own eyes; but what can I say?
O Sa'eed, my heart doesn't have the patience to bear this.

Far from being a remote place untouched until recently by the contemporary world, Afghanistan, as the cliché would have it, has been at the crossroads of history for many centuries, and the Pashtuns who populate the ranks of the Taliban are among the most mobile of its citizens. They constitute, in fact, one of the great trading and service communities of the region, established in large numbers all over India from medieval times and as far afield as South Africa since the nineteenth century. Today the members of this cosmopolitan population may be found between Moscow and London in Europe, all over North America and in the great migrant cities of the Persian Gulf. In fact it is even possible to say that such reality as pertains to the tribal and rural image of the Pashtuns was fostered during the nineteenth century, by the British policy of constituting so much of their homeland into a set of protected jurisdictions as part of the Great Game, in which Afghanistan became a buffer state between British India and imperial or later Soviet Russia. The strange intimacy that exists between the Taliban's remote homeland on the one hand and the heart of global politics on the other is made evident in this poem by Faizani called 'Pamir', that brings together the silent beauty of this mountainous region with the clamour of a very modern war:

I know the black, black mountains;
I know the desert and its problems.
My home is the mountain, my village is the mountain and I
live in the mountains;
I know the black ditches.
I always carry a rocket-launcher on my shoulder;
I know the hot trenches.
I always ambush the enemy;
I know war, conflict and disputes.
I will tell the truth even if I am hung on the gallows;
I know the gallows and hanging.
I don't care about being hot or cold;
I know all kinds of trouble.
I am the eagle of Spin Ghar's high peaks;
I know Pamir's canyons.
I walk through it day and night;
I know the bends of Tor Ghar.
Bangles are joyful on the girls' hands;
I know swords.
Those who make sacrifices for religion;
Faizani, I am familiar with such young men.

LESSONS FROM HISTORY

What is remarkable about the poetry represented in this volume is
the deeply historical consciousness it exhibits. Rather than seeing
the war in Afghanistan as one example of an endless conflict
between Islam and its enemies, however, which is how much of
the literature associated with Al-Qaeda describes it, this body of
material possesses a far more nuanced appreciation of the past.
References to the struggles of biblical prophets against ancient
tyrants abound, whether it is Moses and Pharaoh or Abraham and
Nimrod, and Muhammad's battles with those among his own
tribe who wanted to destroy him, are also mentioned. While such
religious figures have always played an important role in tradi-
tional poetry, they often appear in a very different light in Taliban
verse. Muhammad, for instance, was never seen as a warrior in the
old aesthetics, and figures like Abraham, Moses or Joseph were
more often known for their dreams, miracles and, in the case of
the last, beauty, than for any struggle against tyranny. The Taliban
poets, in other words, are very likely drawing upon the modern

perspectives on these luminaries that were pioneered by nationalist and socialist writers in the twentieth century. But of course more traditional views continue to survive in their verse, which is thus a complex form detached from any purely ideological consciousness, as illustrated in these lines on Joseph's enchantment of Potiphar's wife, as well as on Abraham's love, by a writer with the pen name Majbur (Helpless) from the poem "Abraham's love":

> Not only Zuleikha wanted him, but
> Worlds were astonished by Joseph's charm.

> When he passed from the world,
> The sky and earth were astonished by my beloved.

> However much Nimrod tried to throw him to the fire,
> But by the love of Abraham, the fires were astonished.

> The wisdom of foreigners were shocked by his love,
> Majbur! Words are astonished by your imagination.

Far more important in Taliban poetry than such religious eminences, however, are the military heroes of the Afghan past, men like the great medieval conqueror Mahmud of Ghazni, the eighteenth-century empire builder Ahmad Shah Durrani and the nineteenth-century tribal leaders Akbar and Ayub Khan, who fought against the British during the Anglo-Afghan Wars. A striking absence from this list is Alexander the Great, a frequently mentioned hero in the poetic tradition, and one who had actually campaigned in what is today Afghanistan. Perhaps Alexander's foreign origins now disqualify him from Taliban praise, though interestingly he is simply left out of the *dramatis personae* in their aesthetic and not viewed as an alien invader like Genghis Khan, another great conqueror from the distant past. The patriotic nature of this literature might also explain the importance in it of two women, the seventeenth-century poetess and warrior-queen Nazo, and Malalai, who fought against the British at the Battle of Maiwand in 1880. Both women are Afghan folk heroines, and have been lauded in the past by the nationalists and communists who provide so much of the Taliban's aesthetic with its origins. Needless to say, the behaviour of these courageous women, even as described by Taliban writers, departs in a striking fashion from that officially expected of their Afghan descendants by the move-

19

ment. And the recent history of Afghan struggles against Soviet or American invasion has produced no more heroines of this kind, though the bravery and fortitude of unnamed women who typify the country's indomitable spirit continues being praised in the Taliban's poetry. There do however exist poetesses among the Taliban who take on the personae of Nazo and Malalai, as Nasrat does in the lyric entitled "Give me your turban", which begins with the couplet:

> Give me your turban and take my veil,
> Give me the sword so that the matter will be dealt with.

Seen to date from the anti-Soviet *jihad* of the 1980s, today's war in Afghanistan stands front and centre in Taliban verse. Yet its importance pales in comparison with the Anglo-Afghan Wars, which are seen as the truest test of Afghan endurance and the surest proof of their victory. Unlike the globalised rhetoric of those associated with Al-Qaeda, it is not the defeat of a superpower like the Soviet Union that becomes the chief example of Muslim heroism here, though this is by no means ignored, but instead a colonial war of the nineteenth century that had a strictly regional significance. Apart from demonstrating the patriotic rather than planetary dimension of the Taliban's struggle, therefore, the role played by the Anglo-Afghan Wars in this literature makes of the British an enemy so obdurate as to reduce both Russians and Americans into the palest of their imitators. So if Britain could be vanquished, the reasoning goes, neither Russia nor America ever had much chance of victory. Entailed in this story, of course, is the view that the British in our own time are of no consequence, as the Taliban authors do not make the mistake of confusing their imperial glory during the Raj with today's politics, in which the United Kingdom is seen merely as an adjunct of the United States. Nevertheless, it is not uncommon in this literature for all Westerners to be referred to as Englishmen, thus demonstrating the great hold that colonial narratives still have in the region.

If Mullah Mohammad Omar and the Taliban regime he leads find little mention in the movement's literature, neither do Osama bin Laden and Al-Qaeda, to say nothing of the Arab and other foreign fighters who made Afghanistan their home. And though Taliban verse owes something to the poetry and song associated with globalised Islamic militancy, as seen, for instance, in the description of coalition forces as Crusaders, or in references to Muslim suffering the world over, it is overwhelmingly Afghan in its emphasis, and dispenses with the desert scenes, tents, charging horses and other themes popular with such militants. Also absent from this corpus of verse is the purely religious element, with prayer, pilgrimage or even sharia law seen as being part of a broader cultural landscape and in any case linked to Afghanistan in particular. Here, for instance, is the loving description of a destroyed mosque, its congregation and muezzin by Khalid Haidari in a poem with the title "Traveller Friend":

> You would not ask me what happened to the small
> congregation:
> The grey and dusty mosque,
> The one in the middle of the village,
> The pretty mosque without a door.
> And
> The tender Talib *Jan,*
> The one with long hair,
> The young Talib *Jan,*
> Who used to cleanse hearts with his voice when he called the
> *azan.*

While there are numerous references in the body of Taliban poetry not only to foreign countries like Britain, America, Israel or Russia, but also to particular sites like the White House and the prison of Guantánamo Bay in Cuba, Afghanistan dominates the whole. Even influential neighbouring countries like Iran and Pakistan play little part in the poet's imagination, being viewed with suspicion for the most part or seen as places of bitter exile. Afghanistan is, however, a resolutely Pashtun land for the Taliban poet, with the country's other ethnicities receiving cursory acknowledgement, even as their literary traditions, and the cosmopolitan world of Persian most of all, are on full display in his or

her verse. Yet the fundamental ambiguity and double conscious-
ness of this aesthetic makes for a remarkably diverse set of voices
in Taliban poetry, capable of expressing everything from bloody
vengeance and the thrill of battle to a desire for non-violence
so complete that Mohammad Hanif, with the pen name Hairan
(Amazed) asks God to forbid violence altogether in a poem titled
"Oh God! These People!"

> End cruelty so that
> An ant won't die by someone's hand.

> No traveller will be bitten by someone else's dog,
> And nobody's dog will be killed by someone else's hand.

How are the Americans and their allies seen in this literature?
As we know, they represent only the most recent of many invaders,
of whom the British in the nineteenth century take pride of
place. But this enemy also changes shape a great deal, sometimes
described as a dragon from ancient lore and sometimes as a guest
who ends up occupying one's home. Here, for example, are some
lines from Najibullah Akrami's *Poem*:

> A small house
> I had from father and grandfather,
> In which I knew happiness,
> My beloved and I would live there.
> They were great beauteous times;
> We would sacrifice ourselves for each other.
> But suddenly a guest came;
> I let him be for two days.
> But after these two days passed,
> The guest became the host.
> He told me, 'You came today.
> Be careful not to return tomorrow.'

Whatever form he takes, the enemy is always cruel, and his
immense power only shows up this inhuman cruelty, as in the
following description of a very real and even commonplace inci-
dent, the mistaken air strike (possibly by a drone) on a wedding
party. Complete with an ironic reference to the human rights that
coalition forces are meant to be defending in Afghanistan, the

poem is anonymous and entitled "The Young Bride was Killed Here":

The young bride was killed here,
The groom and his wishes were martyred here.
The hearts full of hopes were looted here,
Not just those two but the whole group is martyred.
The children were murdered,
The story full of love is martyred here.
All their human rights were hurt,
The lover was martyred, the beloved is martyred.
The friends who were escorting them;
Alas, what beautiful youths are martyred.
The bride is drenched in red blood,
Her jewellery is broken and martyred.
Her hands are red with her blood;
Storms came upon her beautiful life.

But the news brings press releases from Bagram,
Saying that 'we have killed the terrorists.'
How can we know the happiness of a wedding?
'We have killed many Afghans today.
This is a threat to our crusade,
That's why we killed those children.'
.They give the fighters' name to the bride,
They say that we only killed our enemies.
The president has appointed a commission once again:
'Go and see who they have killed.'
Their pockets are filled not to say a word,
Because they have killed our relatives
As if the Red Forces came on their houses.

Just as important as the foreign enemy, however, is the countryman who collaborates with him, and whose betrayal of Afghanistan serves as a sign of the occupation's vast powers of corruption. And it is in describing this facet of the war that the Taliban poet adopts a comic or bitterly satirical tone, condemning in particular the creation of ill-gotten wealth amid overwhelming poverty, while describing the new society it produces with some care. Here for example is a poem by Matiullah Sarachawal called "How Many are the NGOs!" Anyone who has worked in Kabul, or for that matter in other post-conflict zones, will recognise the extraordinary accuracy and closely observed detail of this piece. Whatever good work they might otherwise do, NGOs here are accountable to their foreign sponsors, Western governments and international organisations who want to create a "civil society" in such places, rather than to the people they are meant to serve. They routinely hire the friends and relatives of local elites, create a new class of consumers paid in dollars who are disconnected from the local economy, and try to introduce Western norms including letters of reference and women's empowerment in a situation where poverty and disempowerment are the norm for all categories of person:

> Wasting time, they merely sit in their offices,
> How many are the NGOs!
> Their salaries, more than ministers',
> How many are the NGOs!
> Wasting time, respecting recommendations,
> Those who have no recommendations are forgotten.
> How many are the NGOs!
> When you are interviewed, they ask for recommendations.
> During interviews they make tension suddenly;
> How many are the NGOs!
> When there is a vacancy, boys are appointed;
> They will not admit that they are over-aged,
> How many are the NGOs!
> If the applicants are girls, they will be admitted without interview;
> Women in large numbers but men are few.
> How many are the NGOs!
> Most people who broke with the government move to NGOs;
> The reason is, salaries are in dollars,
> How many are the NGOs!
> People come from here and there taking salaries in dollars;
> They don't work in the government because they have their hearts broken,
> How many are the NGOs!
> If someone gets to be head of an NGO, then he is rich,
> So they enjoy a better living situation than Karzai.
> How many are the NGOs!
> Perform the tricks, spend large amounts;
> It is not clear where these people come from;
> How many are the NGOs!

A meddler strolls around with his bodyguards;
That Afghan doesn't think about the situation;
How many are the NGOs!

And here are some lines from another comic piece, titled "Condolences of Karzai and Bush", by an anonymous Taliban poet. This is a dialogue describing the parting of Hamid Karzai and George W. Bush, once the latter ceased being President, as if it were the separation of lovers, a theme very popular in the traditional literature of the region:

Karzai:
Life is tough without you my darling;
I share in your grief; I am coming to you.

Bush:
As for death, we'll both die;
Alas, we'll be first and next.

Karzai:
Give me your hand as you go;
Turn your face as you disappear.

Bush:
Sorrow takes over and overwhelms me;
My darling! Take care of yourself and I will take care of myself.

Karzai:
Mountains separate you from me;
Say hello to the pale moon and I'll do so as well.

Although the verse presented in this volume is concerned by war above all, the diversity of its themes prevents it from being defined as war poetry in any conventional sense. Indeed I have tried to argue that if anything, Taliban verse represents a reaching out to the larger aesthetic tradition of Persian and Urdu, and thus serves to link the Afghan war to a world beyond that conflict, one that we have seen includes not only the mystical and erotic literature of the past, but also the more recent ideologies of nationalism and socialism. And this makes of it an important bridge, both cultural and political, to people and places beyond the ideological realm of the Taliban. Yet nor does this connection entail an attitude of openness to all things. Rather than Islamic law or social conservatism erecting the obstacles to any engagement with other ways of thinking about peace and social order, what is striking about this material is its fervent and very modern criticism of human rights, which is after all the slogan under which coalition forces operate in Afghanistan.

Taliban verse, as I have noted, is full of statements decrying as hypocrisy all invocations of human rights by coalition armies. And the violation of such rights by the Americans or British is viewed as being so egregious as to empty the category itself of any meaning. The accusation of hypocrisy, in other words, is not matched by any desire among Taliban poets to recuperate some authentic form of human rights, and in this way they diverge fundamentally from the rhetoric of international politics. Yet we have seen that these men and women are also capable of expressing their utmost horror at the exercise of cruelty, even when it is perpetrated by their own side, and regularly sing about the virtues of peace, love and harmony in the name of humanity. The great question as well as opportunity sounding out from this literature is how to establish such virtues in a post-war Afghan society without enclosing them in the legalistic carapace of human rights that has been marred from its origins by an association with imperialism. For in the absence of rule by consent, it was often humanitarian considerations that gave Europe's colonial empires their legitimacy in the past.

Nor is it Islamic law so much as the pastoral utopia of some vanished tradition that provides these poets with a way of envisioning a humane society of the future. Naturally this does not amount to much as far as the establishment of a new society is concerned, but it is surely not insignificant that the feeling for humanity pervading Taliban verse is not defined in terms of life. While these poets rue the taking of innocent lives and are outraged by human suffering, in other words, unlike their enemies, they do not hold life as such to constitute some absolute value. Rather it is the exercise of virtues like courage, tenderness and yes, even vengeance, that serves to manifest humanity in their eyes. This way of thinking is certainly traditional, for the Christian West as much as the Muslim East, but throughout the Afghan war it has also become a resolutely modern view, having been linked to the critique and rejection of human rights at a conceptual level. Will the humanity that pervades Taliban poetry be able to instantiate itself in society without the aid of human rights legislation? Or will it eventually have to annul itself in the latter?

Introduction

Ghazi Portraits

"Wars today cannot be won without media. Media is directed to the heart rather than the body. The weapon is directed to the body. If the heart is defeated the battle is won and the body is defeated."

Taliban website administrator, 2011[1]

"[Afghan police officer] Nabi calls himself a patriot and a defender of core values: "I love any song that praises our religion and homeland," he says. And despite the contradictions, like many people he is mesmerised by the nationalistic and religious zeal of the [Taliban's] songs, which also draw on Pashtun folklore and stirring family images."

"Underground Anthems of War", *Afghanistan Today*[2]

"Through their social practice of itinerancy and support from grassroots alms, it seems that [they] were able to write poetry of extreme impropriety, focusing on the primacy of passion as morality. More than that, taliban poets were able to actively lampoon specific local elites from a position of self-deprecating non-dominance, and were often known as wicked satirists."

Robert Canon, "Printed Orality"[3]

We were sitting in a garden in western Kandahar. All around were tiers of pink, purple, yellow and red flowers. It was approaching evening, when the white *de spey gulaan* flower[4] would release its scent. In the centre of a square pool a fountain sprayed jets of water, forming an umbrella, and the air was cooled. All of this is modelled after the images of paradise that occur frequently throughout the *Qur'an*. An educated local government official was telling us about the songs that the Taliban use to accompany their videos.

"These are extremely emotional songs, even for me," he says. "We Afghans are a very emotional people. Even if these songs go against who I am and what I work for, I still feel something in my chest every time I hear those words being sung."

We are in Kandahar, but it might not be the city you recognise from news reports.

The role that emotion plays in the everyday lives of Afghans is not something that comes up often, but often aesthetics are intimately bound up with emotions.[5] It applies as much to those affiliated with the Taliban as it does to those who have nothing to do with the movement.

Glimpses of this other dimension were revealed in Thomas Dworzak's photos of Talibs that he recovered in 2001 from dusty photographic studios in Kandahar, or the many pictures of Talibs with *kohl* applied to their eyes.[6] Usually, however, these images are seen and described as "foreign" or "other". The poems in this collection[7] afford us our first opportunity to engage with the Taliban's cultural output in any significant number in an English translation. We can read them on their own terms, not for their novelty value, but as a way of understanding who the Taliban are.[8]

The very idea of members of the Taliban writing and publishing poetry undermines many of the traditional stereotypes we hold dear about them. These poems offer another means of exploring those seemingly perennial questions: who are the Taliban, and what do they stand for? On some levels the group is extremely secretive, but on others it can be surprisingly easy to talk to those who fight in their name and to explore what they stand for. Indeed what they stand for may not be entirely coherent or even consistent, and may be aestheticised or moralised and differ from what we expect (perhaps a set of political goals, perhaps other objectives), but it is a vision nonetheless. These poems allow us to come into contact with one part of this vision.

At around the time we started working on Mullah Zaeef's memoir, *My Life With the Taliban*, we became acquainted with the Taliban's website and the fact that many poems and songs were published there. While other research priorities occupied us for the next few years, we always made a point of collecting the Taliban's poems, wherever we encountered them, whether online, orally or on cassettes. After some years living in Kandahar, one of the most important lessons we learned was that there was more to who the Taliban are than the stereotype suggests, and that their poetry offered a new perspective on the group.

While monitoring the Taliban's website, we also observed which parts of it other organisations would translate for their own purposes and newsletters. Oddly, the poetry would always be overlooked, presumably because it wasn't deemed to have "operational" value. Yet it seemed to be such a prominent part of what the Taliban wanted to present about themselves to the wider world. This was interesting as much for what it revealed about foreign reaction and interest in them as it did in terms of who the Taliban were.

Indeed, what do the many poems posted to the Taliban's website say about the movement? Where do these poems come from, and why are they worth reading? And why is it important that we ask these questions?

The 235 poems in this collection aim to showcase some of the diversity of thematic and stylistic content as well as offering three dozen older examples from the 1980s and 1990s. These poems are part of a long tradition of Pashtun poetry (although the equally rich Farsi/Dari and Arabic traditions have played their role) stretching back hundreds of years. These older poems mostly could not be characterised as being "Taliban poetry" themselves – in this manner, at least, it is a novel form among this tradition – but the genres, metres, themes, metaphors and emotional appeals used are often similar or the same.[9] It is in this way that we can talk of the Taliban's cultural heritage, one that has a great deal in common with a broader Pashtun cultural heritage.

In the same way that we can say that the Taliban are a movement with many Pashtuns but not a "Pashtun movement", their poetry is a tradition which draws on many inputs from Pashtun cultural traditions but we would stop short of calling it a "Pashtun cultural tradition".

For this collection, the two sets of poems have different provenances and selection criteria. The older poems of the 1980s and 1990s were collated from magazines, newspapers and cassette tapes, transcribed where necessary and then translated. The researcher who carried this out was tasked with gathering a variety of different styles and themes. The newer poems, in contrast, are an almost complete collection of all those published on the Taliban's website between December 2006 and February 2009. In this respect, it is a representative sample of the different styles and themes as found in the post-2001 repertoire of Taliban poetry.[10]

31

For the post-2001 material, there were occasional postings of poems by classic poets like Rahman Baba or Khattak, as well as some by non-Taliban-affiliated amateur authors. These we have omitted. While we find them noteworthy, and their selection for publication on the Taliban's website indicates a certain commonality of interest, we were aiming for a more authentic group of poems, one that was closely tied to the Taliban movement. We will return later to these issues of authorship.

The question of emotional resonance is extremely important for the Taliban: without it, the poems featured in this collection would probably not be read and recited as widely and as avidly as they are. Emotion can be a powerful motivating factor, even for the unaffiliated, and it is often discounted in analyses of who the Taliban are, or who among them does the fighting; their emotional response to the situation around them is a key part of that identity.

These poems cover a wide range of themes, although they often focus on the effects of war inside Afghanistan or on inspiring rank-and-file soldiers to continue their *jihad*. They range from long elegies with reportage-like focus on the details of a single village, to pastoral scenes and reflections on the beauty of a rose, to religious meditations. Most of the poems in this collection are linked in some way to the conflicts that have afflicted Afghanistan over the last three decades. This is especially true of those written post-2001, but the civil war of the 1990s looms large in those written before 2001.

For the most part, the poems are couched in highly personal terms – referring to the things about which one expects poets to write – and where there are political messages, often they are not as overt as one might expect. There are love poems, religious poems, and nationalist poems; many, however, focus on suffering precipitated by the conflict, on the poet's will to fight back, and on why the Taliban are resisting. Additionally, there is a fair amount on the quotidian experiences of villagers.

Many of these concerns are mirrored in a volume recently published from the other "side". *Heroes* is a collection of poems written by British soldiers (and their families).[11] The themes and concerns of these men and women and their Taliban adversaries are remarkably similar. Both sets of poets take leave of their mothers before they leave for the front, both are in turns thrilled and fearful when the moment of battle arrives, and both grieve at the death of friends and family.

Talk to an Afghan for any length of time and you'll find he or she uses a quote or a phrase from a poem at some point during the conversation. Poetry is part of the lifeblood of social intercourse, whether among politicians on late night TV chat shows in Kabul or among villagers in some far-flung province.

Poetry in Afghanistan has a long and rich history. This is as true for Farsi/Dari as it is for Pashto. Rumi is often associated with Turkey in Europe and the United States, but in Afghanistan he is known as either Mawlana or just Balkhi ("from Balkh"). A succession of Afghan rulers sponsored and supported poets like Ferdowsi (who wrote the *Shahname*) while in Herat the Timurids oversaw a cultural renaissance that extended past poetry to tile-work, pottery, architecture, painting and other arts.

The name of the first Pashto poet is unknown, but the first Pashto poetry that we can identify with some certainty is by Bayazid. There were almost certainly poets writing before him, but the two legends of the Pashto poetry tradition are Khushal Khan Khattak (1613–1689) and Rahman Baba (1650–1715). They are still very much quoted, read and recited by Afghans.[12] They were prolific, and the scale and variety of subject matter covered to a certain extent defies summary.

Poetry features in all spheres of life: on political occasions, for social change, for religious purposes, at home, for weddings, for funerals, for festivals and even – as we shall see – on the battle-field. Talk to any fighter from the 1980s war and they will tell you stories of poetry and song. In contemporary Afghanistan, the late Ahmed Wali Karzai occasionally hosted sessions of music and poetry in Kandahar in which the poets – just as they might have done in England's Elizabethan court – eulogised their host.

Afghanistan's contribution to Farsi literature dates back centuries and some features of this esteemed tradition have carried through to this collection. Poets often name themselves in the penultimate line of the poem[13] in an invocation. The forms and rhyme schemes employed are often the same ones that have been used for hundreds of years: the *ghazal, landay* and *sandara* (and so on) are all standard formats with their own rules.[14] Certain tropes have become standard: the image of the moth drawn to the flame, eventually consumed and burnt up; that of women washing their clothes in the river, or collecting water at the well; the allure of eyelashes or bangles jingling on their wrists, and so on. These are all commonplace in Taliban poetry.

Poetry written by religious students – *talib*s with a small "t" – is a tradition that extends as far back as there were religious students:

33

"Taliban (like some other groups such as herbalists or itinerant entertainer castes) were a special and different case. As Ajmal Khattak's memoirs describe it, local landed elites were frequently unable to co-opt or block critical poetry when performed by trans-local taliban. If local maliks refused to allow talib parties a public forum on the taliban's own terms, they could rest assured that their stinginess would become talib lore, defaming their lack of beneficent manhood throughout the countryside.

"This personalised attack on specific powerful people, rather than 'powerful people' as an abstract category, would not be the case with the more ordinary sort of village poets tied to landed power. For them, social criticism seems to have been oblique and metaphorical, taking lyrical form. Of course, the two types of poets did listen to each other, and could not be stopped from informing each other's work. Important as that point is, it is also important to note another thing. Taliban had institutional links to a horizontal, even if highly marginal, network outside the geographical purview of local power; and those links protected them from the control of 'mere' locality. Both Mlatar and Khattak describe their freedom with a great deal of romanticism, at the same time they describe their abject poverty."[15]

Nowadays, poetry and an aesthetic consciousness remain a feature of daily life in Afghanistan. They are perhaps fading some-what – sections of the younger generation may be less aware of their poetic heritage than hitherto – but nonetheless are still widely in evidence.

There are all sorts of proverbs and sayings that are used frequently in daily speech. Sometimes they are used to prove a point, or to spice up or lighten the moment during a long speech. The president uses proverbs as does the baker on the street corner. Well-known poems are often excerpted and used liberally in conversation or in an argument. In Kandahar, there is even a corpus of incredibly sexually explicit sayings that seem to know no bounds.

Folk songs are also part of the tradition. They can be found all over Afghanistan, but there is a particular predilection for them in the southern provinces. We still remember the former mujahed commander with whom we lived who would wake before dawn to intone haunting village tales. The pitch of the voice is high and – just as in the Taliban's *tarana* – the form seems adapted to Pashto rhythms and poems.

Even while there seems to be a precedent for this kind of poetry and cultural output in the south, there are just as many folk songs and ballads in Dari as there are in Pashto. A village might only have one man who knows the old songs (or a woman, among women), but as such they are considered repositories of sorts.[16]

Indeed, in southern Afghanistan it seems poems are sung at the extremes – very late or very early in the day, when death calls, for celebrations and, above all, amid suffering.

Moreover there are dozens of stories which were first recounted in verse but whose narrative has been transferred into folk wisdom and into the repertory of commonplace sayings and tales. Notable among these is the tragic love story of Laila and Majnun which was first popularised in a poem by Nizami but is now a common cultural reference. There are several other variants of this. The classical poetry of several centuries past is also frequently assigned as part of the syllabus studied in madrassas.

Remember, too, that there is also a precedent for this kind of recitation in the *Qur'an*. Islam's core source is told in a *saj'*, or rhymed prose, and is intended to be recited. Recitation is a part of life in that, five times a day, the *azan* calls the faithful to prayer. This increases during Ramadan in *tarawih* gatherings during which a complete recitation of the *Qur'an* takes place throughout the fasting month. Qur'anic recitation often occurs at births, and always for funerals at the *fateha* ceremonies.

The madrassas in Afghanistan and in Pakistan both follow a syllabus, the so-called *dars-e nizami*, that includes the *Panj Ketab* (or "five books" in Farsi/Dari). These books include a translated version of the classical Arabic collection of stories, or *Kalila wa Dimna*. All of these are mainstays of the literary output of the region. Madrassa students are expected to read these books and memorise parts of them.

Every Thursday evening, poets around the country meet in groups to recite their latest works and to discuss what they have been reading. One occasionally comes across them in government offices, like the young man in Kandahar who was looking for an edition of Christina Rosetti's poems. Similarly, each year there are poetry festivals around the country. Two of the most famous are held in Nangarhar and Kandahar: *Narenj Gul* and *Anaar Gul* respectively, named after the orange blossom and pomegranate blossom that flower in spring.

Some poets are so well-known and beloved by Afghans that they are feted as celebrities. Abdul Bari Jahani, for example, was treated as such when he travelled round greater Kandahar in the early winter of 2011–12. These older poets are respected both for their age as well as their wisdom. Poetry remains part of the cultural heritage of Afghanistan's younger generation, something that cannot be destroyed, unlike the Buddhas in Bamiyan, a literary phenomenon marked by idealism and strong convictions.

* * *

Even though it seems strange to talk about the two in one breath, the Taliban have a long association with poetry, from the songs Mullah Mohammad Omar would sing after battle during the 1980s *jihad* to the *tarana* that replaced music on the radio when they ruled Afghanistan.[17]

The "ban on music" that the Taliban are known for having imposed – especially from 1996 onwards – was not a prohibition on *all* music. In the words of the scholar John Baily, this was about "competition between different kinds of music."[18] The Taliban opposed the use of instruments, and permitted only the *daff* or *da'ira* frame drum. Thus, unaccompanied folk song was still permitted, as were the monophonic but melodic intonations of poetry. This isn't something unique to the Taliban, although their increased control over the state – including, by 1996, the capital, Kabul – meant that they were able to enforce it quite easily. The Christian Quaker movement that emerged in the mid-late seventeenth century had similar views on the use of music: resolutely against it.[19]

From an Islamic perspective, there are several competing strands of debate regarding the role of music, which have, accordingly, seen the marker of consensus move both ways in previous centuries. There is no explicit mention or instruction regarding music in the *Qur'an* itself, but the *hadith* collections do include commentaries on the use of music.[20] Different communities have interpreted these sources of evidence in different ways. The Taliban represent one of these strands, informed as they were by the Deobandi tradition they had absorbed through their education, but also by their attempts to project their Islamic experiment outwards to the wider Muslim world; Mullah Mohammad Omar, for example, was highly sensitive to how the movement was perceived by other Islamic countries' governments and peoples.[21]

This was also not the first time music and the arts had been censored in recent Afghan history. During the 1980s, the Soviet-backed Taraki government manipulated artists, musicians and poets in the service of the state; they were forced to perform and produce material suitable for broadcast and for use as propaganda against the "religious reactionaries."[22] In turn, the *mujahedeen* fighters targeted those singing for the government.[23]

The Rabbani government that took power following Najibullah's fall imposed strict measures. Musicians were forced to apply for licences, and when Hekmatyar was appointed Prime Minister he closed Kabul's cinemas and banned music on radio and television. This came after Rabbani's government as a whole attempted to set up an *Amr bil Maroof wa Nahi 'an al-Munkar* – the Ministry for the Promotion of Virtue and Suppression of Vice – institution.[24] In Herat during the early 1990s the main *mujahedeen* figure, Ismael Khan, actually managed to install his own *Amr bil Marouf* enforcers, restricting the use of amplified music as well as the specific lyrics that could be sung by musicians.[25] In the northeastern province of Badakhshan during the same period, *mujahedeen* commanders and local Mullahs censored music and dance in the area.[26]

The Taliban government that ruled over much of Afghanistan from 1996 onwards sought to impose their own standards and rules. Instruments were not to be used, cassettes with songs were forbidden, and the *tarana* became the main aesthetic product associated with the movement. Musicians were forced to sing these on national radio. One example related by Baily has Nairiz, a radio singer in Kabul, agreeing to sing such an anthem. He chose specific lyrics, however, which he said the audience understood properly but that the Taliban failed to decipher:

> "Remember the poor are protected by God
> One day He will answer their cries
> And their oppressors will be punished."[27]

Saraji and Faqir Mohammad Darwish were two of the best-known singers of *tarana* during the 1990s. Saraji cited the subject matter of the lyrics as reasons for their appeal among Afghans:

> "From my experience, the taranas always have profound effects in our society, because the singers often use poems that talk about pride, the motherland, defending the country and the defeat of foreigners in the past."[28]

The ban on musicians and musical instruments was most keenly felt by those living in the big cities with long-standing cultural traditions and practitioners. In Herat, the Taliban carried out a burning of instruments, citing the following *hadith*: "Those who listen to music and songs in this world, will on the Day of Judgement have molten lead poured into their ears."[29] Music has both a long history and a significant following in Afghanistan so it wasn't easy for the Taliban to impose such a prohibition. In December 1996, the *Amr bil Marouf* released the following to Kabul residents:

> "To prevent music. To be broadcasted by the public information resources. In shops, hotels, vehicles and rickshaws cassettes and music are prohibited. This matter should be monitored within five days. If any music cassettes [are] found in a shop, the shopkeeper should be imprisoned and the shop locked. If five people guarantee the shop should be opened the criminal released later. If cassette found in the vehicle, the vehicle and the driver will be imprisoned. If five people guarantee the vehicle will be released and the criminal released later."[30]

Even towards the end of their rule, they were still issuing similar decrees. An order from Mullah Mohammad Omar dated May 1999 addressed what was thought of as the problem of music being played in the Taliban's own official vehicles:

> "The officials of the *Amr bil Marouf wa Nahi 'an al-Munkar* in the entire country are charged with the duty to inspect the Emirate's vehicles. If cassettes of music and songs are found, the vehicle in question shall be seized and be handed over to the office of the Emirate."[31]

Despite these formal edicts, Mullah Mohammad Omar himself seems to have enjoyed music, song and poetry. Reports of this predilection come from interviews with those close to him during the 1980s and when he was leader of the Taliban. Saraji was a particular favourite:

> "Omar had banned all forms of music, but riding in his SUV he liked to pop in a CD of Saraji, a Taliban who has sold millions of recordings of patriotic war chants. Head bowed, Omar would lose himself reciting along:
> 'This is our home, the house of lions and tigers
> This is the land of high mountains and green views and rivers
> And best of all, this is the country of mujahedeen and holy
> martyrs
> We will beat everyone who attacks us
> We are the defenders of our great country.'"[32]

A prominent political and military figure in southern Afghanistan recalled the following anecdote about Mullah Mohammad Omar's music preferences:

"As we drove through a pass between the mountains just behind Omar's land, Naquib turned on the CD player, and the Toyota was filled with Afghan music. I asked if the CD was his or had come with the car.

'It was here when I got it,' Naquib said, opening the CD storage container on the armrest between the front seats. We looked for secular music among the discs of keening prayers, and fiddled with the sound system for a while.

'Are you telling me,' I said, when we had made a selection, 'that this stuff belonged to the man who put people in prison for listening to music?' Naquib shrugged. 'It seems so.' The song that was playing, he said, was a popular Afghan tune that vilified General Rashid Dostum, the Uzbek warlord from Mazar-i Sharif. Its chief refrain was 'O murderer of the Afghan people.'

'What is life without music?' Mullah Naquib said."[33]

Nevertheless, the *tarana* replaced other forms of music on Afghan radio stations in 1996–2001. Here, for example, is a translation of a tape transcription of a song dating to 2000 sung by Abdul Hakim Sajjad:

"Pick up your gun and sword, the time for martyrdom has come today;
Jihad is required for everyone.
Come on, let's head for the trench, today the time for bravery and honour has come.
Pick up your gun and sword, the time for martyrdom has come today;
Either we will return as brave soldiers, or we will lose our heads.
Come on, let's head for the trench, today the time for bravery and honour has come.
Pick up your gun and sword, the time for martyrdom has come today."

After the fall of the Taliban in late 2001, the government that followed it implemented policies that seemed to mimic the spirit of the previous sanctions: a ban on women singing on radio and television, on stage or on the concert platform.[34] A Human Rights Watch report published in July 2003 entitled "Killing You is a Very Easy Thing For Us" describes attacks, rapes and killings of musicians in areas close to Kabul.[35]

Musicians, of course, have far more freedom to operate nowadays than they did while the Taliban were in power. Artists and poets, too, share these freedoms. This all happens alongside the production, distribution and consumption of the Taliban's songs.

* * *

The issue of authorship of the Taliban poems is an interesting one. To start with, there is a distinction to be drawn between the poet and the person who intones a poem on an MP3. Often the poem will be more closely associated with a famous voice rather than the poet himself. Most poems published on the official website list an author although these are usually pen names (you can tell this from the name itself, which will have a meaning – "the *mujahed* on his own" and so on).

Zabiullah Mujahed recently stated that a team of around forty singers were involved in an official capacity, producing around a dozen songs each month.[36] Anecdotal evidence from Kandahar suggests that the verse published on the Taliban's website comes from a wider pool of talent than just this "official" capacity. It is not only active Taliban fighters who can submit lines, but sometime-sympathisers or even just university students. The poems submitted are almost all written in Pashto. The Taliban do not translate their songs and poems from Pashto into Dari or into Arabic as they do for everything else on the website. This is undoubtedly on account of the difficulty of translating poetry, but also because the Taliban's Dari-language *tarana* output often employs a quite different set of formal, rhythmic and aural building-blocks. The *tarana* are also exclusively geared towards an Afghan audience, and sometimes do not appear to target any particular audience at all.

The poems that are published online as verse or in MP3 format as songs are often by those who do not occupy positions of authority within the movement. During the 1990s, poems by these leaders could be found, but nowadays these are less evident. This collection includes three poems by one currently serving senior Taliban leader. The website will occasionally publish verses written by Rahman Baba or Khattak. There is even one poem written by a woman. Needless to say, this is very much the exception.[37]

Aside from the poems written during the 1990s, when we can be more certain of authorship and can tie names to specific individuals, the post-2001 material is far harder in terms of identifying authors. We don't really know in any systematic manner who is writing these poems (aside from circumstantial evidence mentioned above).

The poems are distributed in many forms. Mostly people exchange MP3s using their mobile phones.[38] Shopkeepers will sell videos and songs this way, and it is done among friends. Then there are the poems published on the official Taliban website. Other poems are published as books; these are mostly the non-political examples. The MP3s are also used as ringtones on phones; again, this is quite common and isn't just something found among Taliban affiliates or supporters.

One clue that helps in identifying the nationalities of those involved in writing the poems are references made to specific locations or aspects of the conflict. The poems presented in this collection are representative of the kinds of *tarana* that the Afghan Taliban produce. Regardless of the fact that most were gathered from the official website, this is apparent even from an initial read. There is, however, an entirely separate Pakistani production line that seems even more active than the Afghan equivalent. The Pakistani anthems produced are more broadly geared towards capitalising on their strict propaganda value; unlike their Afghan equivalents, it seems the messages are finely tweaked and nothing is distributed without some kind of official sanction and/or manipulation. This may, in part, reflect the somewhat different manner in which the Pakistani Taliban operate and are structured, but further research would be needed to confirm this.

Reading into the biography of an author from his or her creative output is fraught with problems and the difficulties are compounded when discussing Taliban poetry. It is hard to confirm the identities of authors, and there is a wide range of individuals represented in the cross-section of poems presented in this book. Only very few writers submitted multiple poems during the period in which we were collecting them.

Note, too, that during the compilation of this book some poems were identified as having been written by individuals who are definitely *not* affiliated with the Taliban – a provincial governor, a reporter for the Voice of America news service, a Kandahari student, and so on. These were identified by chance, and it is possible that others will be identified following publication.[39]

It is uncommon for the authors of *tarana* to become famous on the basis of their work; rather, those who recite the MP3 audio versions gain some measure of celebrity for the quality of their voice. This is also in part a corollary of the oral culture that

41

exists in much of Afghanistan, and explains why authors embed their name or pen-name (*takhallus*) into the poem itself lest their authorship be forgotten or lost. The sound and presentation of the poems as songs are an important part of how they were intended to be consumed. Although the texts are presented as texts online, the MP3 download part of the site has greater prominence and is updated more often. The songs, when sung, are always monophonic, unison melodies. The singer is always a man (or a boy), never a woman. The words "hypnotic" or "trance-like" are often employed by foreigners to describe these audio versions but seldom by Afghans themselves.

The melody lies at the upper edges of the range that performers are comfortable with singing, which lends a more intense and heightened quality to the melody. The use of reverb effects added in post-production often add an echo. As such, the musical quality of the songs themselves is distinct and almost immediately recognisable upon hearing a few bars of an audio track. Sound effects "from the battlefield" are occasionally added, but this seems to be more common among the Pakistani Taliban than among Afghans. The *tarana* are frequently used as the soundtrack to propaganda videos showing attacks on American or Afghan forces that are mostly produced and distributed out of Pakistan.

The *tarana* released by the Taliban in Dari sound quite different from those in Pashto, in part because the music and rhythm inherent in the sounds of the language are quite different. Even without understanding a word of either Dari or Pashtu, distinguishing the two is quite easy.

Traditional Pashto poetry forms predominate in the songs and almost all of them are written in a traditional style; there is very little that could be described as "free verse". The rhyme and rhythm are also traditional for the most part and any Pashtun would have been exposed to them in his/her childhood or adolescence. These poems and the forms they inhabit are also the same forms used in the 1980s, operating with the same conventions. The *ghazal*, for example, has a repeated end-rhyme which recurs at the end of every line, but not at the half-line or *beit*. Note, too, that while these *tarana* are consumed in the city, they remain a product of the rural or village culture from which the Taliban movement emerged.

The audience that listens to these *tarana* in Afghanistan is large and diverse. We have observed both young and old, male and female watch or listen to some version of them,[40] even members of the government. Remarkably the key to their success may be the

42

seeming absence of any spiritual or political agenda manifested in many of the poems.

Quite often, while sitting in a room with friends or acquaintances, passing the time, someone will inevitably pull out a mobile phone and show you the latest video of a Taliban attack or of a beheading, all set to the soundtrack of a *tarana*. Villagers will have the raw audio on their phones. Afghan television channels will often screen long excerpts from such videos. Indeed, in the cities, the videos and the audio tracks form a large part of some people's exposure to the Taliban. Both Jere van Dyk and David Rohde – kidnapped and held across the border in Pakistan by groups associated with the Taliban – reported an obsessive fascination with these songs and videos among their captors.[41]

* * *

The poems are, for the most part, relatively straightforward in their meaning. Some of the imagery is intelligible only to someone with prior exposure to Pashtun poetry, but almost all of it is comprehensible by any audience (even a non-Afghan one). There is some symbolism, but the poets draw from a relatively standardised canon of imagery, while the situations described make deciphering the meaning somewhat easier.

It may come as a surprise that the word "Taliban" is employed infrequently in these selected poems although there exist several synonyms used to denote those affiliated with or fighting for "the Taliban". One of the most common of these is "mujahed", or "person who does *jihad*"; "ghazi" is another word that is frequently used.[42] Sometimes the poet seeks to address a broader audience so he/she will reference words designed to appeal to fellow Muslims ("brother", "umma" and so on). The language used to describe those fighting inside Afghanistan in the section "The Trench", for example, implies broad alliances: "mujahed", "Muslim", "Afghan" and so on. This is symptomatic of the Taliban's aspirations to be at the forefront, as a national movement, of resistance to the Afghan government and the foreign forces. Often – and this is more characteristic of the personal poems – the author will simply refer to his "trench friend", or "brother" and so on.

The poems are not uniformly positive, however. "Quatrains" speaks out at the grinding, repetitive nature of the conflict:

"Alas, Afghans don't know how to go forward;
They are slipping backwards into dust."

The author of "Self-made Prison" locates the problem even closer to home:

"It's a pity that we are wandering as vagrants,
We did all of this to ourselves."

The international forces are the single most visible group referred to in the Taliban poems. The poets draw upon a rich admixture of complaints, denominations, slurs, descriptions and attitudes in writing about the foreigners, who are generic, there being hardly any distinction drawn in terms of exactly which country they belong to. Little attention is paid to "the Americans", as is sometimes the case when talking to Taliban affiliates and fighters. In some of the poems, care is taken to be deliberately oblique (for poetic effect). Aside from criticisms of NGOs and humanitarians – portrayed as having aligned themselves with the foreign military forces, in any case – there is no mention of a non-military foreign presence in Afghanistan.

The two poems that refer to internationals in the pre-1994 collection presented here offer strikingly opposite attitudes. "Blood Debt" is strident, and amid a catalogue of international involvement in Afghanistan states:

"The Pharaoh of the time sends arrows everywhere,
These arrows will finally strike Washington's chest."

The other, "Message to the Internationals", offers an appeal to the foreigners:

"Now we look at you with hopeful eyes,
We are begging before you.
Why did you become like Pharaoh?
Why are you concealing your nose?

Why don't any emotions come to your heart?
This is essential for human beings.
O enemy of ancient humanity,
This is one of your moral duties."

For the most part, unaffiliated Afghans – those not fighting – are referred to as victims of some sort. The portraits that emerge are of people going about their daily lives only to find them disrupted or destroyed in some way (usually by foreigners or just in general, by the conflict).

In "This Oppressed Orphan Belongs to Which Martyr", the poet decries the anonymity of so many of the conflict's victims:

"The orphan, who has been burnt in this censer,
Has been torched in the flames of loneliness
It seems like he has been torched in flames
His heart seems to have been pierced by arrows
He is a captive in the chains of oppression and cruelty
He screams, he screams."

One of the most interesting things about these poems is the fact that the Afghan government (in its various forms) features hardly at all, even though our collection from 2007 onwards is relatively representative. The satiric dialogue between Karzai and Bush ("Condolences of Karzai and Bush") criticises what is seen as fawning obsequiousness. "Slave" addresses Karzai directly:

"Karzai! You sold the country for a few dollars.
As you are a wrong-doer, to whom should we complain?"

"How long?" explores the economic conditions in the country brought about by the local government:

"Pretending to carry out reconstruction; they established personal businesses,
They enjoy life, and you? How long will you wander in the rubbish heap?"

Another relatively common theme is Guantánamo. The imagery of prisons was already a rich vein dating back to the 1980s *jihad* – in which some of the Taliban's poets will have fought – but Guantánamo has renewed this thematic store.[43] The US detention facility at Guantánamo Bay continues to provoke strong emotions inside Afghanistan (as outside).[44] The same holds for Afghan prisons as well, of course, but a definite collection of symbols has emerged around the Cuban prison, from the orange jumpsuits to the loneliness of prison life on an island and so on.[45] Even within Guantánamo itself, there was (and presumably remains) a size-

45

able group of poets. Mark Falkoff has collected some of these in the essential *Poems from Guantánamo*,[46] although there are no Afghans represented in this collection. Detainees who have since been released tell of informal poetry recitations, while Mullah Zaeef opens his autobiography, *My Life With the Taliban*, with a poem that recalls Guantánamo.

Within the canon of Taliban poetry one can usually discern when poems have been deliberately written for the purposes of propaganda or when they are simply submissions from poets and from those lower down within the movement, unaffiliated with the formal messaging apparatus. There are, broadly speaking, three kinds of Taliban poems in this sense: those with a clear propaganda message, officially sanctioned; those very close to the same line and inciting others to fight, but unaffiliated with the propaganda apparatus; and completely unaffiliated individuals.[47]

When all the poems are taken together, however, their sheer range of reference and sourcing is remarkable. While not all included in this volume, poems published on the Taliban's website cover most trends of Pashtun political and literary representation from the twentieth century; even the Communist PDPA is featured through the works of Suleyman Laiq. Indeed, it is this eclectic spread that brings out the aesthetic and political continuity with wider parts of Afghan society.

The collection of poems was categorised as follows:

Before September 11 – Here we have gathered some poems that were written by Talibs or their affiliates prior to the September 11 attacks as we wished to contextualise the poems that came afterwards in terms of both subject matter and style. We begin with personal accounts, find poets who have been drawn and pulled into war, move on to descriptions of battle and salutes to fellow fighters and then swiftly run up against victims of war. There are some that directly reference the Taliban movement, some messages to the international community from that time as well as some anthems about the nation.

Love & Pastoral – The poems from 2007 onwards begin with more lyrical offerings: descriptions of gardens, feelings of separation from the beloved, as well as a poet's invocation to action.

Religious – Perhaps surprisingly, there are relatively few overtly religious poems in the collection. Of course, religious imagery and references are made throughout, yet only a few of the poems are exclusively devoted to such themes. This section begins with prayers and invocations, moves onto poems about those who stray from their religion, as well as those who remain on the path, some relating to Ramadan and *Eid* and some others.

Discontent – Poems expressing dissatisfaction about several topics, among them the feelings poets are experiencing, how writing helps them deal with their discontent, unhappiness with the actions of women, the behaviour of fellow Afghans and poems expressing these feelings in a national context. Finally, there are some poems responding to the foreign presence.

The Trench – These are the Taliban's war songs. Obviously, many people within the movement have been active on the front lines and these poems give some sense of their experiences: from bidding farewell to their families, motivational chants before battle, descriptions of "the enemy", descriptions of fighting itself, of night raids, of pain, of martyrdom and of remembrance. There are some nationally and internationally framed poems relating to the conflict and the section ends with a series of fighters' self-portraits.

The Human Cost – Much of the collection is concerned in some way with the suffering that the conflict has precipitated. The section begins by examining this theme this on a national level, moving on to torture and the prison experience, general descriptions of pain, prayers, expressions of defiance, descriptions of orphans and children, and the suffering of villages; it concludes with poems about graveyards, funerals and death.

* * *

In early 2011 it was suggested that the US military should consider responding to the Taliban's *tarana* in kind via some sort of "counter-poetry".[48] Needless to say, an attempt to instrumentalise or "weaponise" poetry for the purposes of fighting "the cultural war" is probably not something the US military ought to be engaged in. In a way, there is nothing to instrumentalise here. It is like the discussions in the media debating the existence of the "Taliban's Twitter account" through the second half of 2011 – focused on the ephemera but failing to engage with the real substantive issues involved.[49]

Of greatest significance about these poems is the fact that they represent (for the most part, and as far as we are aware) uncensored voices from within the Taliban. Not all of the poems may come from the Cultural Committee itself, but, by posting them on their website, they come with their own unique form of endorsement. Thus this collection of poems is, by that token, one of the only ways we have to begin to comprehend the thoughts and feelings of a wider selection of those involved in the Taliban, beyond the occasional individual interviews and formulaic press releases. Indeed, this volume represents the first time so many voices from the Taliban have been given expression in a manner that is not confined to what we might term the purely political, or the purely religious. Nor are these poems something that the Taliban might wish to censor in that they manifest and express part of who they are. This is not politics, but identity.

The perspective that they bring is a new one. It is one that allows the reader to appreciate those who comprise the Taliban as human beings (regardless of what actions they may have taken), and, as such, shed light on who these people actually are, and what they stand for as individuals.

The variety of voices manifested in these poems allows us finally to escape from discussing Afghanistan only in terms of policy or security matters. The poems, each the expression of individual sentiment, endow the poets in question with agency, responsibility, and ultimately accountability as well. As such they prompt us to rethink our assumptions about a movement that has perplexed outsiders for decades.

Before September 11

I am still talking

Like a candle, I laugh in public and cry in secret,
I can just chirrup like a scream and then I disappear.

If the enemy is trembling and escaping from me,
He would certainly do it while I am being buried.

But listen to this speech of mine and understand that
I am still standing even after my death.

If I seem to disappear
I will always appear in the mind.

I will not become dry like grass,
I am still talking with the pen's tongue.

I will teach you a lesson as an example,
God willing, you won't forget it.

Abdul Basir Ebrat
Written during the 1990s

Waiting

I spend my nights hoping for you,
I spend the long nights in waiting.

I, cupbearer at your doorstep,
Still spend the poisonous cups of separation.

Always, in your grief, towards my shirt,
I cause a cascade of lukewarm tears.

Broadcast on the radio; author unknown
Written during the 1990s

The Troubled Shepherd

Your flute's sound is nostalgic,
O shepherd, troubled with the world's civilisation.
As you spend the nights by yourself in this dusty desert,
Your business is the song with flute, O shepherd.
Your old hair and dusty beard look very heavy,
O shepherd, unaware of time.
May *Allah* make the wolf disappear, the jackal that would trouble
    you,
O shepherd, away from home for months.
May your songs' poems not run out on the journey,
May you not be hungry in the desert, my dear.
Who will tend to your cracked feet and rough hands?
You haven't seen any blessing or comfort, O vagrant shepherd.
Shoemakers are tired of pounding nails into your shoes,
You didn't find new shoes, O shepherd without beauty.
You seem to have understood the secret of mortal life,
O disbeliever in the world of materials, shepherd.

April 1998

My God

O God, I cry out loud for you,
I beg your forgiveness of my mistakes.
In order to reach this destination, you created me,
A destination that I am surprised to go to.
It is a pity that from the courtyard of this transient world
I am leaving with the carpet of a lifetime of my sins.
My, Sahar's, sins are less than your blessing.
If you forgive me, I will be very proud.

Bismillah Sahar
1998

Prayer

I have opened my mouth in prayer,
You have brought down your blessings
In order to make my body blessed,
To have the problems resolved.
The spot on my heart makes a candle like the sun
To watch the earth and skies with.
Flower my hope's blossom with your blessing,
To perfume all directions with its smell.
Make me a translator in the gathering of mysticism,
Fill my speech with secrets.
Bring my mind beyond words,
Show me the gradation of minds.
Barialai's lap of fear is full of hope;
He has brought a gift to be blessed.

Abdul Ghaffar Bariyalai[50]
Written during the 1990s

Beauty

There was a sun escorting your beauty,
There was a moon with you and a great army of stars.
The ignorance of the dark turned to light when you came;
The army accompanying you dug into the chest of darkness.
You brought us cups filled with modest fruit,
As you had the mountain of modesty and patience's mine with
    you.
All these good qualities are mixed up in you;
You have Jamshid's cup,[51] Khotan's fragrance[52] and Haidar's
    voice.[53]
Minds are surprised by it;
You have the art that has amazed leaders.
Few inhabitants have presented good gifts;
I, Ebrat, am presenting this mind as a gift for you.

Abdul Basir Ebrat
1994

Thunder

I am looking for wishes in the darkness of life,
I am looking for my hopes mixed in among the soil.
The treasures of my wishes disappeared over time,
That's why like Majnun: I am looking for deserts.[54]
Affected by lukewarm tears,
I became a sea of mourning; I am looking for storms.
My feelings became upset with the feelings of other citizens
I am looking for a cure for the mind's thunder.
The courtyard of my love was ruined in the earthquakes of the
    time,
I am now wandering, looking for other courtyards.
The garden of my imagination was baked in the oven of cruelty,
I am looking for pain in imagination.
I, Ebrat, either went mad or have eaten hashish,
I am looking for flowers in thorns.

Abdul Basir Ebrat
1994

Dedication

In whatever accent I ask
Of the very white stars of this sky
On the state of my absence from the beloved at home
They would tell me in a few short words.
They give me the message of his life again,
They tell me he passed from this line.
Look for him up in the heavens,
He left because of these frustrations.
Like a holy and love-struck imagination,
It reaches the whole world in a flash.
Watch out, he has been inspired by the butterfly,
As he reaches the sky over the hot fire.
I understood that he has walked a long way,
Today they have lit candles on every slope.
They have taken out the pillars again,
They have buried darkness for every dark moment.
Watch out my beloved away from home,
Each Farhad is sacrificing his head for you.
With every drop of your red blood,

Angels are making dots out of them.
You are like a candle, turning yourself to ashes,
With the intention of lighting this gathering.
You have bought death at the cost of life,
With the intention of reaching the high target.
Today, on every stone,
There are traces of your red drops.
I see your image in every home,
There are still songs left in Shakib's heart.

Sardar Mohammad Shakib[55]
April 1998

Mujahed of the High Mountains

As the breeze of dawn spreads,
As the light opens its eyes,
A [wisp of] smoke at the side of the tent
Comes dancing up.
From that village above
The sound of the *azan* comes[56]
The doors of hearing open:
He will get up.
The wind spreads sweet song,
Adam secretly with his nice lips
Whispers prayers.
He wears a turban on his head,
He goes up to that spring,
He takes his ablution, splashing.
He goes to God's home then.[57]
He stands respectfully.
He then raises his hands for God,
O *Allah*, O *Allah*,
Keep me victorious always.
As the sun spreads gold,
He goes back to the tent.
He puts on
Ammo vests and chains.
He then moves.
He puts his finger with pride
On his dagger.
With every step

The chains of bullets clink.
The wind blows at
His *patu*'s drooping corner;[58]
Under the *patu* it reveals
The black barrel of his gun.
He bows down with pride,
Then looks up and straightens his back.
He takes a few steps back,
Then looks at the tent.
At the front of the tent,
Pearls fall down
On the green woollen veil.
After that with crying,
This song is whispered.
O *mujahed* of the high mountains,
Give your *salaam*s to the wind, it brings them to us.

Ezatullah Pezhand
2000

Change

The spring of change needs blood to rain down,
It requires the irrigation of the gardens with blood.
Valuing the blood of the people of the past
Requires the price of human blood.
Each drop of it has become a Nile of the dawn's blood;
The Pharaohs want to fill the Nile with blood.

Bismillah Sahar
Written during the 1990s

Warm Poems

O pen, these cold chests ask me for fire,
They want to put our houses in hell.

The bride of independence is not for free,
This bride requires a few heads.

This wild night won't be lit up by a few stars,
Be aware my friends, it wants a sun from me.

It will never grow green with the winds of autumn,
This seed of hope wants spring from me.

As it didn't bring its head on shoulders to us,
That heroic neck now wants necklaces from me.

The tree of my lover's beauty cannot be irrigated with just a few
    drops,
O tears, flow, because it wants this flow from me.

For the ice that is still in the minds of the tribes,
O Ebrat, it wants the warm poems of emotions from me.

Abdul Basir Ebrat
Written during the 1990s

Dawn's Light

We will break the hands of the dark night
Wishing for the white dawn.
We will give them a floral breeze in exchange,
Wishing for the disappearance of the smell of blood.
Our blood will become a flower on every dewdrop,
Hoping to find the lost martyr.
We are not free for your breezes, O spring!
We are still looking to spill blood.
We won't disappear even if we are cut into pieces
Seeking your crying, O enemy.
Our beauty, Miraj, became love.
I, the lover, am hoping for his visit.

Abdul Qayyum Minawal[59]
April 1998

To the Wayfarer

O, my homesick and exhausted lover!
You still need to walk to reach your pretty house.
This world full of darkness
Seeks your red blood's hue.

In the gloomy nights of this old prison,
A few of those oppressed are still in handcuffs.
There is hope for you to the east,
There are still a few heavy wolves to be found.

The silent storm in the sky's heart still
Seeks to put out your zealous candle.
The scary flashes of clouds
Want your wishes to rot.

But you do not care and with open chest
Go to your target and hit a stride.
With the sharp sword of grand intent
You cut the head of any rebel storm.

This brings tremors to the high mountains,
Brings tremors to the enemy's heart.
On the cold chest of every friend,
Brings encouraging warm fires.

Abdul Basir Ebrat
Written during the 1990s

Trench Friend

May my head and property be sacrificed for you, friend,
O my trench friend.
May my heart's flesh be sacrificed for you, friend,
O my trench friend.

May I be sacrificed for you – may I be sacrificed for your faith,
You are close in the trench, my faith in you grew stronger,
O my trench friend.

You take on tanks – you go with pride,
You don't fear the artillery or tanks of the enemy,
O my trench friend.

On the storms of the time – on the floods of the time,
You don't care about them, may you be as strong as mountains
     against them,
O my trench friend.

In the bosom of red flames – in the bosom of storms,
You like them, you have the morals of the butterfly and the sea,
O my trench friend.

In the roar of earthquakes – in the roars of storms,
The echoes of your honour are spread all over,
O my trench friend.

O my brave friend – my dawn's friend
May your turban not fall, my turban-owning friend,
O my trench friend.

Bismillah Sahar
May 2000

Discomforting Path

It becomes like a hot furnace for me,
It gave me hard troubling blows.
It gave me hot fires in my heart,
O life, create great pains.
These small pains aren't painful enough,
I am happy in fire just like the butterfly.
The storm's wave doesn't shake me,
I came to the battlefield with renewed intent.
I have prepared for your fight,
I am hoping to change my destiny.
I have passed through a very discomforting path,
I would either get to the peak of the mountain
To bring the red flowers of love from there,
Or I would lose my head
To bring martyred hopes.
My hopes pointed to me to move

While they were dying.
The drops of tears in the crying voice
Shouted a few times for me:
Look at these fires,
Take care not to stop walking.
The destination is close, don't worry about us
Where there is grief, there is laughter afterwards.
My great God, may you cut them into pieces,
As they cut our poor country into pieces.
I, Ebrat, have become tired convicting them,
Much less me, even the pen got bored.

Abdul Basir Ebrat
1994

Martyr Friend

He, on the edge of taking leave of life,
On the edge of the path of continuous silence,
He who would win hundreds of breaths,
By giving out one breath,
Yes,
At the cost of a free independent life,
The youth who got love's inspiration from a butterfly,
He slept beside the burning light,
He got burnt, he did business with his head.

Mullah Abdul Wali Halimyar
1998

I will be commending your history

O hero of Spin Boldak, I am proud of your deeds,[60]
O Martyr Hafez Abdul Rahim, I will be commending your
    history.

Just as your waves were stormy in resisting the enemy,
Just as you would make dread shouts at him from all over,
O my beloved, I will seek you out on doomsday.
O Martyr Hafez Abdul Rahim, I will be commending your
    history.

History became a shining activity on your forehead
Every scene was witness to your heroism and honour.
Your memories are left with me, I am crying.
O Martyr Hafez Abdul Rahim, I will be commending your
    history.

You were taking one thing as a gift to your beloved,
Well done with your zeal, your name is left for Afghans.
I inherited your trench, I am pulling up my sleeves,
O Martyr Hafez Abdul Rahim, I will be commending your
    history.

Your attack was against the enemy who was arrogant,
Your emotions were in your soul as you always had motivation.
I will take your revenge from your enemy and be victorious,
O Martyr Hafez Abdul Rahim, I will be commending your
    history.

Congratulations on your dignity and that you reached your goal,
You wore the blood-coloured shroud and were sacrificed for the
    right love,
I, Mozamil, am standing crying on your shrine,
O Martyr Hafez Abdul Rahim, I will be commending your
    history.

Mohammad Zaman Mozamil
Transcribed from a recording made during the 1990s

O Hero Youth of the Time

I salute you, O hero youth of the time!
I salute you, O oppressed companion youth!
You are the possessor of great zeal,
You are full of zeal.
You are the voice of brotherhood,
You are full of bravery.
You give your head for your honour,
This is your nature.
Many heads fall,
With every blow of yours.
Every enemy shook,
With your Haidari blows.[61]

Signs of Khalid are apparent
In every action of yours.
Every flower is smiling,
Every blossom laughs.
Every coming day dances,
All that is dark was crying.
Blackened and dried lips
Were opened by every blossom.
Here, the palace of the wild,
It reached as high as the sky.
The happy life's hope was
Tired and frustrated.
As your thunder came down upon it,
It was destroyed and demolished.
Every martyr's tomb,
Dances and twirls.
The red drops of blood again
Bring colour and make beauty.
The lukewarm tears of the orphan,
Became stars and are lightening.
You consider the songs of freedom,
For every living creature.
You read the lesson of independence
To every human being.
Maidens, for the hopes of Ebrat,
Go to youthful desires.

Abdul Basir Ebrat
Written during the 1990s

The Lost Friend

You were unaffected by my exile,
My dear, I haven't sought you enough.
You killed the light of life,
As the butterflies didn't challenge you.
I would see your troubled image in my dreams,
You wouldn't leave me when awake.
Separation from you dried my eyes,
You were not blessed in the holy bosom.
In this sad journey of looking for you,
I haven't remembered you in every place.

61

The stubborn people didn't light
Candles for your separation.
The cupbearer didn't clang
The empty cups of water to serve you.
It has been months and years since your separation,
I didn't miss you much yesterday.
O my northern prison-afflicted friend,
I haven't asked about you from the enemy.
The poor Mutma'in so far
Hasn't kissed the soil yet.

Abdul Hai Mutma'in
1998

Hopes Empyrean

It's enough; don't light disunity's fire anymore
In this ruined and poor village.
Listen to those mourning screams,
They echo in the village to the west.

O enemy, bear this in mind,
Their earthquakes of zeal commence.
Or a storm of conscience will arise,
Or oppressed screams will become thunder.

Watch out, the flood of tears is out of control,
Watch out, the sea of blood became bloody.
Listen, it became like a great sea, its waves
See that cruelty's maelstrom is being destroyed.

God willing, darkness' heart will explode
When dawn's eyes shine.
The eye of time will flinch
When the sword of our zeal is shown.

This oppressed nation's drops of blood,
Boiled in clamour and uproar.
It is breaking these steel handcuffs,
These Pamir youths became motivated.[62]

Either the thunder of hate will fall on him
To burn your sinister wishes,
Or in my Kabul Jan's mountains[63]
Your hopes will flow.

The new breeze brings new colours.
God willing, we will climb to the heights of hopes
With green velvet on our shoulders,
With a burnt carpet of the dusty land.

Ebrat's pen will be dancing to it,
It will be writing *ghazals* of laughter.
Spring breezes will blow again,
The flowers' faded lips will smile again.

Abdul Basir Ebrat
Written during the 1990s

I am crying for your martyred face

You are cut into pieces, I couldn't recognise you,
I am crying for your martyred face, O you, soaked in blood.

It became Karbala on your behalf for the young and the old,[64]
They were all suffering for your loss, the healthy and sick.
The universe screamed while your blood was flowing,
I am crying for your martyred face, O you, soaked in blood.

Yazid has come to the field and tormented dear Hussein,
They have torn the ropes of mercy's cradle from our hearts.
Wolves were among the herd, autumn was felling the leaves.
I am crying for your martyred face, O you, soaked in blood.

There would be stories like Hajaj and the oppressor's attacks on
    you.[65]
What a flood of blood was made; the sky's sides were red.
All stars took on the soil's colour and there was a solar eclipse[66]
I am crying for your martyred face, O you, soaked in blood.

I became insane in my love of you and crazy in your memory,
I became a stranger to my relatives in the waves of grief,
God knew that salt was being poured on my heart.
I am crying for your martyred face, O you, soaked in blood.

Stop, stop the story, O Nasim, stop crying,
In this period of pity, stop talking about cruelties,
O Hamid, clean up your tears, you suffered a lot.
I am crying for your martyred face, O you, soaked in blood.

Hamidullah Hamidi
Transcribed from a recording made during the 1990s

The Nation's Murderer

O murderer of the nation, why do you bring grief to Afghans,
You deserve hell, you will be going to the hot flames.

Paradise's smell is *haram* on you,[67]
O murderer of the nation, why do you bring grief to Afghans,
You deserve hell, you will be going to the hot flames.

All the hells are ready for you, go,[68]
O murderer of the nation, why do you bring grief to Afghans,
You deserve hell, you will be going to the hot flames.

May you turn blind and deaf,
O murderer of the nation, why do you bring grief to Afghans,
You deserve hell, you will be going to the hot flames.

You fight with some and inflict blows on others,
O murderer of the nation, why do you bring grief to Afghans,
You deserve hell, you will be going to the hot flames.

May you be sacrificed for the Muslims,
O murderer of the nation, why do you bring grief to Afghans,
You deserve hell, you will be going to the hot flames.

Allah has complimented them in the *Qur'an*,
O murderer of the nation, why do you bring grief to Afghans,
You deserve hell, you will be going to the hot flames.

You kill Muslims and have become a bloody murderer,
O murderer of the nation, why do you bring grief to Afghans,
You deserve hell, you will be going to the hot flames.

What will be your response on doomsday?
O murderer of the nation, why do you bring grief to Afghans,
You deserve hell, you will be going to the hot flames.

Don't kill the Taliban, may you get night blindness,
O murderer of the nation, why do you bring grief to Afghans,
You deserve hell, you will be going to the hot flames.

The angels call out damnation to you,
O murderer of the nation, why do you bring grief to Afghans,
You deserve hell, you will be going to the hot flames.

As you have martyred the Taliban,
O murderer of the nation, why do you bring grief to Afghans,
You deserve hell, you will be going to the hot flames.

God will punish you on doomsday,
O murderer of the nation, why do you bring grief to Afghans,
You deserve hell, you will be going to the hot flames.

You are fighting against the holy *Qur'an*,
O murderer of the nation, why do you bring grief to Afghans,
You deserve hell, you will be going to the hot flames.

One wouldn't do this, may your hands be cut,
O murderer of the nation, why do you bring grief to Afghans,
You deserve hell, you will be going to the hot flames.

May God cut you with His own sword,
O murderer of the nation, why do you bring grief to Afghans,
You deserve hell, you will be going to the hot flames.

Widows and orphans are pleading to God against you,
O murderer of the nation, why do you bring grief to Afghans,
You deserve hell, you will be going to the hot flames.

May you yourself get in trouble with it,
O murderer of the nation, why do you bring grief to Afghans,
You deserve hell, you will be going to the hot flames.

As you have trapped your own people,
O murderer of the nation, why do you bring grief to Afghans,
You deserve hell, you will be going to the hot flames.

As you have tormented Gawhari,
O murderer of the nation, why do you bring grief to Afghans,
You deserve hell, you will be going to the hot flames.

They have signed on your foolishness,
O murderer of the nation, why do you bring grief to Afghans,
You deserve hell, you will be going to the hot flames.

Abdul Rahman Gawhari
Transcribed from a recording made during the 1990s

My God

Is this a hell or a world, my great God?
Is this loyalty or cruelty my great God?
As blood is seeping from my heart,
Is this a flood of cholera, my great God?
As I am suffering from the flames of accusation at all times,
Is this a competitor or a friend, my great God?
Tears are flowing due to the severity of pain,
What kind of test is this, my great God?
As laughter leaves my mouth fast,
Which enemy's evil prayer is this, my great God?
As I, Ebrat, became an enemy to my friends,
Whose unfortunate dawn is this, my great God?

Abdul Basir Ebrat
1992

Dissent

Dissent bruised my face with slaps,
Dissent brought turmoil upon us.
The flood of grief struck our homeland,
Dissent turned our copper dishes to clay.
The misfortunes warned us,
Every resident of ours saw dissent.

The spring took away the lap of unity from us,
Dissent spoiled our healthy heart.
Who, from which direction did this dealer leave?
What made the dissent more vivid than sun?
What movement of the vicious has begun,
Such that has made dissent sweeter than honey?
I, Ebrat, would anyway condemn it now,
As dissent has passed the ball of luck away from me.

Abdul Basir Ebrat
1992

Ancient Caravan

Our Kandahar is full of holes,
People are wounded all the time in Zabul.
Battles of zeal took place in Ghazni,
People are burnt in Wardak.
The enemy's roots were turned to smoke in Lowgar,
Youths in Paktya once again have grand intentions today.
Every cunning person was sliced into pieces in Paktika,
Heroes have traveled to Kabul.
Hopeful hearts are encouraged in Helmand,
All wishes are resolved in Uruzgan.
Comforting breezes are blowing in Farah,
The time of thorns passed, and valleys turned to flowers.
The enemy's life was half a day in Nimruz,
Their weak trenches were ruined in Shindand.
The necklaces of happiness reached Herat,
Those without care in Ghor are now paying attention.
This ancient caravan is going around the whole world,
No matter whether Tajik, Uzbek or Mongol.
The gatherings in Ghondanu were cancelled,
The nightingale sings in Bulbuli.[69]
May you wave the white banner in Shamshad,[70]
O great God! This is Ebrat's wish.

Abdul Basir Ebrat
May 1999

Victory's Sun

The sun of success has risen in the sky of victory
My Emirate's soldier has come up to the trench.
Dawn tells of the good news of life,
The sun-lit dawn has come upon the blossom of the gloomy
    night.
It falls on the enemy from their high roof of arrogance,
The swordsman with sword in hand has risen in the east and in
    the west.
We are faced with thorny ways in this thorny time,
The wounded have risen on the hill.
They ruined the palaces of oppressors everywhere,
Akbar's name has appeared on every Talib's sword.[71]
The white rays of his success are spread by every sun,
O Hasyal, doomsday has come upon our enemy.

Abdul Wasi Hasyal
May 2000

Possessors of Honour

The whole country benefited from security
Thanks to the *mujahedeen*.
O zealous father of the turban-wearers,
Your turban will always be high.
If we were daubed red with blood in your honour,
The possessors of honour kept your honour.
As your sons of this period are Sahars,
You are lucky, lucky, O lucky one.

Bismillah Sahar
Written during the 1990s

Sad Sun

On whose face did you appear again?
O upset, sad sun!
O herald of new life!
O dawn of every oppressed man!
Your rays are shining,

They are shining, stormy.
They became a revolution,
They are tearing at the gloomy hearts.
O dagger of the dawn,
Basil is smiling for your rays.
Basil is smiling, the world is smiling,
The mourning Afghan is smiling.
O beautiful shining army,
The great shining army!
There were gloomy nights,
Dark nights spread out.
The sky's skirts were red,
It is because of your white forehead's power
That half the Afghans are out.
There is freedom in your bosom;
There is freedom, independence.
You have brought happiness,
O message of great change,
O leader of great movement,
O competitor, don't be mistaken,
Don't be mistaken, don't be defamed.
Don't become a protester,
It's the poetic inspiration of Ebrat,
Each of his words is a jewel.

Abdul Basir Ebrat
Written during the 1990s

A Time is Coming

A time is coming, a change is coming,
A revolt of white banners is coming.
A white caravan of turban-wearers is coming from all directions,
They have the beautiful light of justice in their hands.
They are going to break the horns of the cruel stranger,
The message of release from colonisation is coming.
A revolt of white banners is coming.

I dreamed last night that Evening was handcuffed,
Dawn was standing in front of it with its sword.
I interpreted its meaning after much effort:

69

Their foreheads would be burnt instead of ours from now on,
Tomorrow is coming in our clothes.
A revolt of white banners is coming.

This situation is giving me the good news,
The dragon's forehead will be broken by the Muslim's sword.
The flames of revenge are fired up in all hearts,
The Amu here and the Euphrates there started churning[72]
A chapter of history, a change is coming.
A revolt of white banners is coming.

Maiwand is watching the new sacrifice,[73]
Ayyub has come for Malalai's honour and support.[74]
Among the swords' clangs and the hail of arrows
The beautiful Laila of freedom is shining her beauty,
The Talib is half-drunk for her, approaching like Majnun.
A revolt of white banners is coming.

Once again it is the time of light, darkness is passing,
There are clangs of the white dawn's swords in the darkness.
It will take the dark cottage of darkness away,
O Sa'eed, our dawn is overcoming the darkness again.
See the evening, it comes poor, weak and scared,
A revolt of white banners is coming.

Sadullah Sa'eed Zabuli
Transcribed from a recording made during the 1990s

The Islamic Movement's Forces

They install white banners on the high mountains,
The Islamic Movement's forces advance.

They are on the right path climbing on the *batil* house[75]
The Pharaohs of their time will be drowning in their waves.
They are like the storm against the Prophet Noah: it cannot be
    stopped by dams.
They pass over the high mountains and like a wave over the
    dams,
The Islamic Movement's forces advance.

All the youths have risen out of honour and zeal,
They have come to the field of sacrifice cordially.
All Afghan emotions are triggered,
The tribes of the homeland have risen with one voice.
The Islamic Movement's forces advance.

They will reach their destination, little time is left,
God's orders will be implemented all over Afghanistan.
Mountains and hills of the homeland are encouraging in this,
The ominous plans of our enemies will come to aught.
The Islamic Movement's forces advance.

This ruined country of ours will be built,
Darkness will turn to light.
The palaces of the oppressors will be destroyed,
The cruelties against the oppressed will come to an end.
The Islamic Movement's forces advance.

Hejratullah Mahjur
1996

Blood Debt

Today, I write history on my enemy's chest with my sword,
I draw yesterday's memories on today's chest once more.
Malalai wants a red spot by her lover's blood
So as to embarrass the rose in the heart of the garden.
Moscow still owes us our blood,
I write the terms of my debt on the chest of the arrogant.
They will ride the white horses in the red field,
Then we will install the white banner on the Kremlin's chest.
The day of red blood will become red with the Red's blood,
The knife that is stuck into the Chechens' chest today.
My enemy, go and read the history of heroism,
There is a page written about Macnaghten's chest.[76]
The Pharaoh of the time sends arrows everywhere,
These arrows will finally strike Washington's chest.
If anyone looks with the evil eye towards my deserts
They will find fires on their gardens' chests.

I, Ibrahimkhil, am on the path of a chosen destiny,
It's no problem if I face difficulties on my way.

Abdul Matin Ibrahimkhil[77]
May 2000

Message to the Internationals

O residents who ride time now,
Pay a little attention to me.
O people who ride on the shoulders of luck,
Pay a little attention to my house.

An incurable heart disease,
Every human here has cholera.
It has dropped on every stone here,
A world of blood passed here.

Unholy hopes were burned here,
Ominous wishes were burned here.
Our hopes in the foreigners' hopes,
Smiled and laughed silently.

Our target was cleared in that house,
We happily rushed over there.
Dead emotions were stirred,
Shining thoughts stared at them.

But alas, when we got close to the destination,
All of a sudden
We faced a calamity
When we lost our faces.

Now we look at you with hopeful eyes,
We are begging before you.
Why did you become like Pharaoh?
Why are you concealing your nose?

Why don't any emotions come to your heart?
This is essential for human beings.
O enemy of ancient humanity,
This is one of your moral duties.

Why do you consider yourself free of it?
This is a part of this world.
May you get blind, pay attention to it.
Isn't this a line of Asia, Herat?

Why don't you see it? Don't you have eyes?
What is happening to us?
Look at it carefully, O big-eyed idol,
What is happening in this country.

Either go away from me, leave me to my business,
In order to build my country by myself,
Or come close to me and honestly become my friend,
And put out the years-old fire within me.

Abdul Basir Ebrat
1994

May I be sacrificed for you, my homeland

May I be sacrificed, sacrificed for your high, high mountains,
For your flowerlike chest and pines.

May I be sacrificed for you, my homeland, each region of yours
    is beauty,
Each of your stones are rubies, each bush of yours is medicine.
Each village of yours is a trench, and every youth of yours is
    sacrificing for you,
Each mountain and hill of yours is a calamity for your enemies.

May I be sacrificed for your dusty deserts and green valleys,
For your flowerlike chest and pines.

May I be sacrificed, sacrificed for you; I will sacrifice my head and
    property for you,
I will give you my body's blood in order to make you fresh and
    thriving.

I will murder all the enemies of your religion and prosperity,
I will gradually make you the holy necklace of Asia.

May I be sacrificed, sacrificed for your hot trenches,
For your flowerlike chest and pines.

May I be sacrificed, sacrificed for your Helmand, your chest,[78]
For your mountains, Uruzgan, your Kandahar-like trenches,[79]
For Zabul's trenches and Ghazni's honourable battlefields[80]
For Gurbat, Gurbat Wardak, Maidan and Lowgar.[81]

May I be sacrificed, sacrificed for your great youths,
For your flowerlike chest and pines.

May I be sacrificed, sacrificed for you while my homeland, Kunar
    is alive,[82]
Your youths from Paktika and Farah are heroes.[83]
Your people from Nangarhar and Laghman are successful,[84]
You have trained famous sons.

May I be sacrificed, sacrificed for your dry ruins,
For your flowerlike chest and pines.

May I be sacrificed, sacrificed for your Hindu Kush and
    Mahipar,[85]
For your Shamshad, Shah-i Kot, Spin Ghar and Tur Ghar.[86]
My ditch-filled country! You have trenches all over.
Your body is Maiwand, Maiwand, you are Habibi's beloved.

May I be sacrificed, sacrificed for your burnt wounds,
For your flower-like chest and black pines.

Habibi
Transcribed from a recording made during the 1990s

National Anthem

It is shining, the land of mysticism,
This is the homeland of Muslims.
It's the beloved homeland, Afghanistan.
It's the beloved homeland, Afghanistan.

We have a good beautiful history,
We have great, great *Ulemaa'*.[87]
We have the enthusiasm of
Ahmad and Mahmud for Independence.

It's a land beautified by the *Qur'an*
It's the beloved homeland, Afghanistan.

We have our fertile soil,
We have gold in our mountains.
The Haidari sword in our hand,[88]
We have Omar's intent.[89]

We will build our homeland again,
The beloved homeland, Afghanistan.

We defeated the warrior Genghis,
We then turned Russians into pieces.
We are getting knowledge and doing *jihad*,
Our sword's blow is sharp.

It's the land remembered by every Afghan,
It's the beloved homeland, Afghanistan.

We have a good shining life,
We have the good right name, "Afghan."
Each of our enemies is escaping,
We have our God and faith.

This is the land of heroes,
It's the beloved homeland, Afghanistan.

May it live forever, it's a champion,
O God, it's like a flower.
May it be united,
Always, Always.

Author unknown, but possibly by Abdul Basir Ebrat
Written during the 1990s

Excited Waves

I hear songs of my power
From the silent mouth of Amu,[90]
In the strong sounds of Kunar,
From the high turban of Pamir.

There are excited waves of Tarnak,[91]
There are roars of Helmand's waves,[92]
There is the straight neck of the Hindu Kush,
There is the scary image of the wild.

Every desert here
Is full of the enemies' heads.
This is the house of heroes,
This is the nest of lions.

The great subject of my freedom is
The wide valleys of Khyber[93]
The high ditches of Panjshir[94]
The meagre forests of Kabul.[95]

This blood on every bush,
These graves every few steps,
This is my proud history,
These ruined walls.

Abdul Basir Ebrat
Written during the 1990s

I am Afghanistan

The whole world knows me from the past,
I am Ariana, Khorasan, I am Afghanistan.

This great feeling that I feel,
It is because I am a hero of the time, I am Afghan.
I am Ariana, Khorasan, I am Afghanistan.

We know very well what to do with each other,
It's none of your business if I am poor or rich.
I am Ariana, Khorasan, I am Afghanistan.

I am not just an empty stone lying on the ground,
I am Abaceen, coming towards you gradually.[96]
I am Ariana, Khorasan, I am Afghanistan.

When it comes to affection, I am a pleasant breeze,
When it comes to hardship, I am a strong storm.
I am Ariana, Khorasan, I am Afghanistan.

Take care not to play with wounded hearts,
I am someone's heart's wish as well.
I am Ariana, Khorasan, I am Afghanistan.

I have no guilt or any crime, but I am being burnt for nothing,
What a strange test plagues me!
I am Ariana, Khorasan, I am Afghanistan.

Possibly by Abdul Basir Ebrat
Written during the 1990s

Love & Pastoral

Freedom

What is the good of Majnun alive when Laila dies?
What is the good of a hollowed-out body when someone's heart
    dies?
The heart is a lamp inside a muddy frame;
May it not pass that this lamp stops shining.
If the bird has flown the cage, the cage deserves to be broken;
If the heart dies, the hollow chest should die first.
The permanence of a living thing is never possible;
When the heart dies; the body has to die and it will die.
Freedom is the heart of each nation's body;
Without it, both the nation and eternity die.

Abdul Shukur Reshaad
December 4, 2007

Soul

The village seems strange; this is separation
as if my beloved has left it.
The grief of separation is so cruel that it is not scared of anyone;
When the soul does not leave the body it shakes.
Like a flower withering in the autumn,
Autumn has now come to my love.
I remain alone with my shaggy head of hair
Uncomprehending; my heart has been sad for a long time.
In a flash, it put a hole in my entire world;
Each affair is like an arrow.
Oh Faqir! Better be sad.
Who told you that love is easy?

Shahzeb Faqir
December 23, 2007

Quatrain

My heart took leave of this world today
Because my competitor took my beloved from me by force.
I will be crying from now on, with red eyes,

Because of the taunts of the neighbours and the neighbourhood.
My beloved! I became mad in your grief;
Because of that, my body bursts into flames.
For God's sake, don't be cruel to me!
Don't be so proud, you won't have this goodness forever.
I, Ghamgin, am mad in your love;
How can you expel me from your home?

Ghamgin

Zeal

Your love aside, what else is there?
It is like approaching the desert.
Like the dust on your footsteps.
Look! The crazy one lay down.
In your love up to the sky
Means rising up from the earth.
Those who burn with the fire of zeal
Are shackled at this time.
Your cheeks in the spring,
Red like flowers.
Admonisher! Give us advice!
My head has burst.
With the heart, I behave correctly with everyone,
But they cheat me.
Your eyelashes never miss
When they are turned against someone.
Your looks have grabbed my heart,
Its heart's habits are like that of a thief.

Pordel Bustan
December 23, 2007

Great Guiding Star

When you were born, time brought changes;
Stars were falling on the earth, beauty brought colour.
Spring arrived everywhere, red blossoms hugged each other
As you brought the love from love's world.

Time's bosom was filled with the light of the maidens;
The moon became the maidens' veil and took the flowers into its
bosom.
Cruelty decamped, barbarism ended;
All the spiritless gods fell down before God's *ka'aba.*
As you brought the lit torches from the upside,
Faith spread to the corners of hearts.
You brought the bells of the way for life's caravan,
A smile spread to dry and dusty lips.
You brought lessons from the garden of love;
Monotheism's rays dispelled the darkness from Mecca.
As you brought "*iqra*" from Hera's cave;[97]
Dark night's heart was torn by dawn's swords.
You brought light and mornings in the hands of the sun;
You enlightened the dark houses with candles of truth.
You brought light to the black hearts of the evenings;
Oh great guiding star! The leader of humanity's caravans!
You brought the message of arrival
To the collection of the beauty, light and gaps.
You brought many gifts of beauty and colours;
The idol temples shiver out of the light.
You brought the order to worship the only God.

Amanullah Nasrat
October 28, 2008

Spring has come

Spring has come, come and break up the grief;
Let us watch each step of power.
It is nothing else but real beauty and art;
It appeared in forms.
How long will you be lying in the corner with your weak body?
Open your eyes you poor Zahid.[98]
Come out! Here there are new shows;
The collar of the buds is to be torn.
Beauty puts the step of the sincere on the eyes;
Flowers left the cradle of dew.
Saqi! Pour some water into the cup
So that it makes us unconscious at once.
Moth! I have good news for you, come to the garden;
The unfortunate beauties have survived.

Rishad! Did delicate things make motions?
The zephyr kisses the cheeks of the flowers.

Rishad[99]
December 23, 2007

New Year

O New Year, bring happiness with you!
Bring the fragrance of flowers.
Once again, spread spring in my life,
Once again, bring bouquets of red flowers with you.
Make my life full of colour;
Bring the colourfulness of the colours with you.
The sweetness of Laila and Majnun's memory,
Bring some of these things with you.
Light the spaces and bring colourfulness,
Bring red flowers and growth with you.
Perfume the air and turn it to spring,
Bring the restfulness of Farah with you.

Farah Emtiaz

Sunset

It is late afternoon and the wind speeds up and then stops;
It brushes against the pine needles and makes a low noise.

A yellow ray among a few branches of crowded tree,
Will shine in the forest just like a candle.

The fast wind makes the branches of the trees hit each other;
Rays of sunlight go back and forth, they don't remain in one
    place.

The nightingale sits on the last branch of the pine tree;
He is very tired, has gone to sleep and is singing very slowly.

The leaves of the trees make a simple music for him;
The nightingale is singing and leaves are moving around in all
    directions.

The pine tree with its strong structure bows and straightens its
   head back;
It hangs its branches loose down its face, and dances while
   standing on one leg.

Evening the twilight arrives slowly with its lap full of red flowers;
Pink rays are spreading over the blush of sky.

Everyone becomes a spectator of this scene for a few hours;
The sweet moments of sweet life pass very fast.

The last moment of this short ceremony is sunset;
Participants at this gathering return when the sun has set.

The sun is like a spirit in the colourful mixture of late afternoon;
When the sun leaves it, they don't stay with each other anymore.

This yellow late afternoon is an example of sweetness in life;
When the spirit leaves, everything is left behind.

Abdul Hai Mutma'in

Learn!

Learn to speak with a melody like the nightingale,
Learn the silent dialogue of the flower with the nightingale.
Cover your head, come out of the blossom,
Learn to blow like a breeze through the air.
How long will you live like a bird?
Learn to fly free like an eagle.
Speed up, make the caravan go fast, the destination is close.
Learn to project your voice like a bell.
Leave comfort and take up hardship, O zealous Afghan!
Learn to cry for the homeland's pain and grief.

Abdullah
September 8, 2008

Religious

Prayer

O owner of beauty and beauties,
I have a request for you,
I raise both my hands towards you.

I pray with humility,
I want to be kept away from disgrace,
I want this world from you.

But you know very well, O God,
For these tiny, tiny Gods on this earth,
Telling truth is considered a sin by them.

So now, guide me what to do:
What should I do with the mouth given to me by you?
Should I either cut my tongue or break my mouth?

Which one of these two should I do?
I should either take up stones or a sickle?
I am afraid to become a fire and be burnt.

The world has become a hell for me.
Where should I go, where I should I buy a house?
How much should I bear, O my Lord?

How much more pain should I carry in my heart?
You are patient, you wait for them.
If you give me power and I take control,

You will see in one moment.
I will take revenge from the enemy of humanity,
There is a flame in my heart; I am being burnt.

I am being burnt every moment
In this fire, fire people.
I am being burnt without any guilt.

O my God! Those people are in control.
They want to eat humans, O my God!
These whales have opened their mouths.

They eat them because of their faith;
May I be sacrificed for you, my God.
Fulfil this wish of my mine, O my God.

With your generosity,
Save your good worshippers from the dragons;
Send thunder down onto them

Or bring down the sky upon them.
Humble these wolf-like humans;
Humble these dogs in human clothing.

Fill this world with roses,
Temper the thorns so they won't hurt the humans,
Make the world colourful with roses.

Make this pleasant world beautiful,
So it changes to a paradise with a drop.
Make the world colourful with love.

As far as the West, East, North and South.
I want a world of love, love;
My throat is full of the bitter smoke of gunpowder.

Make the world as sweet as sugar,
From the darkness and gloom,
Make this world light with your generosity.

Take control of the darkness and bring light,
Bring the stars of the sky to our neighbourhood,
Dedicate some butterflies to us.

Bring cholera to those people,
It tortures me every single moment:
My God, this grief is persecuting me.

Due to this crazy world of yours,
Craziness is biting at my neck;
In the past it was the role of the wild beast.

But now humans bite humans:
They are not content with their dignity.
Out of ingratitude they bite the sky.

Their power made them forget your power.
The rich bite the poor;
Show your power to them.

Show the fires of hell
To the scorpions of this world;
Show the house of the dragons to them.

You have such power and strength,
Such that the human
Even can't imagine.

They can't find it despite looking for it.

You have spread this carpet of earth,
You have raised the sky without pillars,
You have no defect.

This whole world isn't more than a mosquito to you;
If you want, then
Every Nimrod will be careful.

But you don't want and you give them opportunity,
Anything they want, you give them;
You give them all the comforts of paradise.

You give them complete things in this world;
Giving and taking is in your control, O God:
Don't become upset, no matter how it is.

You gave this tongue to me
With which I now ask: what is this, God?
Some are so wealthy.

Some are even in need of shrouds,
Some swim in rivers of wine,
Some others' drinking water as their hearts' blood.

Some lamps can run on water,
Others cannot be lit with oil and are put out.
My God! Don't be upset with me, I apologise.

You know what you do, but the reason I cry is that
Your enemies are covered with blessings.
How long can I be proud of my hunger?

I don't mean myself, God;
I don't count being selfish in humans.
The problems of the world are

The responsibility on my shoulder, O God.
Fulfil this one wish of mine, O God,
My compassionate, my merciful God:

This difference among humans,
That one is on the earth and another in the sky,
Take this away with your power or take

My conscience, my feelings.
I, Shirinzoy, request this, O God,
The God of beauties:

I raise both my hands towards you,
I pray with humility.

Shirinzoy
August 23, 2008

Prayer

I can't compliment you with my tongue,
    I can't write it with a pen.
I can't draw your picture,
    I can't compliment you.

You are aware of all places
You are present everywhere

You lit up the sun,
    out of the darkness of the galaxies.
You made the stars of the sky beautiful;
    their examples are to be found around the universe.

You brought the humans knowledge
You made him God's caliph

Whatever your purpose was,
    I don't understand it.
This was either health or sickness,
    I don't understand it.

But those of you who made them knowledgeable
They destroyed all our places

If you consent to destruction,
    Destruction is in opposition to knowledge.
Or if it's one human killing another,
    then killing is in opposition to knowledge.

You are kind to all
You are the power of the entire universe

If this is correct, then,
    why is there so much difference in this world?
They build the ruins,
    so why is there ignorance in this world?

Or it is intentional revolt
Or somebody has made the insurgency

This we don't know,
    or your consent may be with it as well.
It is due to deficiencies and unawareness,
    or your philosophy is there in it.

We are your creatures as well
We are surprised

Build our land once again;
    give us power and honour in our homeland.
Build Afghanistan once again;
    we can't beg anymore.

Give power to those who are serving
Whatever He wants, happens.

Everything is in His power and control
Whatever He wants, happens

Tassal
September 8, 2008

Ghazal

Separation's warmth is very tough,
Great God, face me with goodness.
This is a mad torment,
Great God, face me with goodness.
I am walking on a path filled with thorns,
I have to reach my destination.
I am very poor,
Great God, face me with goodness.
There is no condolence or brotherhood,
Goodness and faithfulness are lost.
Everyone cares just about himself,
Great God, face me with goodness.
Some people chose mentors for themselves,
Some expect others to help them like
The enslavement of prisoners.
Great God, face me with goodness.
They are migrants in their own country,
Nobody asks about the poor people.
There is obligation, obligation;
Great God, face me with goodness.
Don't defeat the conqueror,
Oh my dominant God.
Life is very dry and tough,
Great God, face me with goodness.

Azizullah Ghalib

Collapse

O God, keep me from hell's fire;
I am a poor creature, don't look at my sins.
I am the guilty and you are too kind;
I have nobody besides you.

You gave me the right way as an inheritance,
But I am weak in front of Satan.
Strengthen me in my fight with Satan;
I will go to the grave under your protection.
I ask for your forgiveness;
I stand in front of you with bound hands and bare head.
I, Aziz, won't count on anyone else,
Even if this world collapses around me.

Azizurrahman

Cry to Allah

O my Possessor, I am thinking about myself;
I cannot withstand any of Your examinations.
When I am healthy, I am higher than the earth;
Arrogance brings me up to such a position.
I forget You and Your compliments;
I either listen to myself or to a rich man.
To one who is higher than me in money or power,
I stand with respect in front of these people.
I always have thoughts of money and wealth in this world;
So when I go to Your place,
I don't know what I am saying when I pray;
I don't realise that I am standing in front of God.
It has become like a custom or hypocrisy;
Show goodness to me because my faith is in danger.
But when a slight sickness or disease comes my way;
Then I open my mouth toward the sky.
When there is no treatment to be found in the world,
At that time I ask for Your aid and kindness.
O God, I can't make my mouth ask You;
I am very ashamed, so I can't ask You.

Eftekhar Ali Fagar

I don't care

If I am put in danger, I don't care.
If my body is split into pieces, I don't care.
They turned our maidens' hands into soil and ashes;

If my head is cut from my body, I don't care.
I leave my property and head for Islam;
If my muscles are fried in the fire, I don't care.
O! My God! Accept my prayers.
If I spend my life in jail, I don't care.
I won't depart from God's Love;
If this Love bursts into flames, I don't care.

Zia ul-Islam

Great God!

Great God! I thank you a thousand times;
The life of the ungrateful is always poor.
What is human in being able to avoid committing sins?
With Your mercy he is kept from committing sins.
Still, you are healthy, you do your prayers and worship God;
Because if you get ill then you won't enjoy things.
Don't be proud of yourself, consider what you are;
Otherwise you will face a calamity.
Pride is deserving of the great God for He is Great;
He is the Lord of the entire world.
Daudyaar says I never conceal the truth,
Even if I were to be hanged like Mansour from a gibbet.[100]

Daudyaar
December 4, 2007

Praise

Feel a little pity for my situation, O God,
Cheer up my sad heart just this once.
It is You who created the universe;
Nobody but You has this ability.
Everything in the world will collapse;
Only You will not fall down.
Make us rich by uniting together;
I have raised my hands in this prayer.
A calamity has reached my tired life:
Save my family and I.
O God, I only have one wish;

When will I join You?
How should Akrami compliment You?
My God, You are unparalleled.

Najibullah Akrami

Praise

O God! I am astonished by Your works;
I am astonished by Your powers.
You created the garden
And I am astonished by the flowers.
You created the sky and the earth;
I am astonished by all these things.
O God! Grant us happiness;
I am astonished by tragedy happening elsewhere.
I hope for security;
I am astonished by this time of trials.

December 23, 2007

Strange Times

These are strange times, people are separated;
Majnun and the mad one are separated from Laila too.
Relative apart from relative, and friend fed up with friend;
The beloved and the lover are separated from the sweet-hearted.
They pretend to worship God, but in their hearts they seek to
    spread the word about others;
I swear by God that they have separated from *Allah*.
By worshipping material things, the worshipper himself became
    lost;
They detach from sister, brother, mother and father.
We lead and are busy with the world but turn our backs on
    religion;
For that, consciousness separates me and you.
I saw the son of a sheikh and a holy man in the cinema,
So his sister and mother left out of shame and modesty.
Oh God! Why? What happened? Am I dreaming or awake?
Giving his love to those of lower status, my brother separated
    from me.

My dear mother! Rise up from the grave;
My step-mother caused me to break from my father.
What is the meaning of a shared life without meaning? An animal
is better than that.
I separated; in fact I separated from a dragon.
These selfish silly people; the lovers of money will come to their
senses
When they hear that so and so silly ones detached from this
world.
When the apprentice is without zeal and the non-believer comes
from within the family,
Teacher! Not only from you, but they separated from their
father.
This is the process of separation; some go this way, some go that
way;
Some break with unfaithfulness, some from faith.
Erfaan! If this is correct, separations will take place a hundred
times;
It doesn't matter who broke with you and who you broke with.

Erfaan
December 4, 2007

Where did they go?

Where did he go? The one who was much loved by God.
Where did he go? The one to whom the *Qur'an* was divined.
Where did go? He who wished that every human would be kept
away
From the fires of hell? He who always yearned.
Where did the last Prophet go?
Where did he go? The one who prophesied the End of Days.
The one who believed in the pious God.
Where did he go? The one who was in love with pious almighty
God.
He stretched his voice to each corner of the earth.
Where did he go? The one who always was concerned with *jihad*.
He devoted property and his life to the name of Islam.
Where did he go? The one who was firm in his faith.
He dedicated his wealth to Islam's coffers.
Where did he go? The young man called Sediq.[101]
All the *kuffar* trembled at the sound of his name.[102]

Where did he go? The young man called Omar.[103]
His generosity is still remembered.
Where did he go? The servant of the pious *Qur'an.*
He honestly served the holy *Qur'an.*
Where did he go? The one called Osman who was very generous
and rich.[104]
The clang of his sword was heard elsewhere.
Where did he go? The one who was called Lion Ali, the man of
the battlefield.[105]
He dispatched many of the *kuffar* with his sword.
Where did he go? The one who succeeded on every battlefield.
Always saying *Ahad Ahad.*[106]
Where did he go? The historical battlefield figure.
He who experienced the lethal cruelties of the *kuffar.*
Where did he go? He who he was called black Bilal of his time.[107]
The companions of the prophet were the butterflies of religion.
Where did they go, the servants of the messenger?

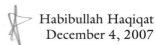
Habibullah Haqiqat
December 4, 2007

They invite

In public they help out;
Behind the scenes they do other things.
They take advantage of people's poverty;
They look for an opportunity for conversion.
They muddy the water and the fish;[108]
They invite people to convert to Christianity.
They interfere in our country;
They have set fire and are watching.
The *kuffar* always hatch plots;
The Muslim is asleep and sleeping.
The Muslim never accepts other religions;
These are just rumours spread by people.
O God! Ruin those who sell their religion;
Kamran is always praying.

Mohammad Nabi Kamran

Regret

What grief and reproof would the person have,
He who is a resident of my neighbourhood's safety?
The maze of the current times is very strange;
Some people receive happiness and others grief.
Be very careful and look to the end,
Whether it is taking a step, using a pen or taking an oath.
There is no benefit for a usurer from his charity,
Even if he becomes as generous as Hatim.[109]
Zealotry is a part of faith, did you know?
Those without zeal will be used as kindling in hell.
Martyrs will be fresh and wet with blood;
The freshness of the flower relates to the amount of dew.
Nobody expressed their condolences with us,
We bear our grief with closed mouths.
For the justice of Islam, only this proof is enough;
They are all equal, whether they are Arabs or the *A'jam*.[110]
Weigh this on the scale of justice, O Hamdard;
It is either a clay pot or a cup.

Habibullah Hamdard

Think about it

Servant of God! Think what you are created from;
You possess wisdom, heart and eyes and still are blind.
You stopped obeying God, you stubborn man;
Why don't you think about it when you are put into the grave?
Realise the reality of your existence;
You are the follower of Mohammad.
You have been called the best in the *Qur'an*;[111]
You are the best of the rest of the *Umma*.[112]
First, learn all of this and then take a step;
God has prevented you from committing any sin.
Oh silly Rashid! If you want God to forgive you,
Then ask Mohammad to mediate if you are wise.

Rashid
December 16, 2007

Selling the faith

Decisions are made there, above in the sky,
No one can be blamed for what happens.
Everyone's fate is separate,
Each man is passing through a time of testing.
One person is granted wealth and selfishness,
One is hopeless from poverty.
Some have sold their faith for money;
They accompany the non-believers elsewhere.
Pious God!
Eliminate their hypocrisy!
Grant a little modesty and zeal to Muslims.
Halim sitting and praying asks that
Muslims be granted dignity in all things.

Abdul Halim
December 16, 2007

Take care!

Keep yourself from the frauds of the cheaters,
Keep yourself from the friendship of the low-bred.
To win and to lose are both damaging;
Muslim! Keep yourself from gambling!
Afghans have always been independent throughout history;
Keep yourself from the slavery of strangers.
O leader! Don't cheat your nation,
Stay away from deception!
Carry out your affairs patiently,
Always make sure not to be impatient.
If you can't keep yourself from taking and handing out bribes,
Stay away from government posts.
If your faith is endangered,
Stay away from unemployment.
You are obliged to make a living,
When you are young make sure you have a job.
O Omar! Obey the Prophet,
Don't obey the devil!

Mohammad Omar Kheywawal
December 16, 2007

Separation

I fell into the river of isolation and separation;
My head is underwater and am moving down the river.
I am looking for an exit; show me.
I don't know what to do in Your absence.
The cruelty of the cruel has fallen on me,
Someone has fried me on the spit of the fire.
I can't accept Western rules;
I have a good clear system in my *shari'a*.
God's law is the path of my life;
I distinguish the East and the West.
My religion, Islam, can't countenance cruelty;
I am the Afghan of the moment and I am hiding.
I am not anyone's slave; I worship my God;
I bow my head to him at the *mihrab*.[113]
O Nadir! There is a spring after each fall;
The flowerbuds of the homeland open at the revolution.

Nadir
August 8, 2008

Take care

God has given you a beautiful body;
Look at what you are created from.
It has been created from the soil:
You have been created for worship.
Today, it is your turn;
You have lost yourself adoring the transitory world.
You even have forgotten who you are;
Moreover, you prefer cruelty to goodness.
You have always oppressed the poor;
You are not sincere in your worship.
Satan accompanies you.
Extreme pride means you keep your hat in your pocket;
You always perform your prayers without a cap.[114]
While worshipping, pride is forbidden;
Why do you feel so selfish?
You can't stand steady during your prayers;
Your body itches all over.
Sometimes you scratch the back of your neck or your scalp;

You are used to this.
Is this prayer or time-wasting?
Or, do you only pretend to pray and instead deceive people?

December 16, 2007

Ramadan

Ramadan is the month of God's blessings;
Ramadan is the month of the heart's mysteries.
Ramadan is dearer to me than anything else;
Ramadan is the month of colourful blessings.
I like the *Eid* of this month;
It is a month of beautiful memories.
The night of *Qadar* is the best of all;[115]
It really is the month of rewards.
Haqmal always likes ramadan;
Ramadan is the month of several philosophies.

Fazl Ghani Haqmal
September 8, 2008

Eid

How can we celebrate *Eid* when our warriors are hungry?
Our homeland's maidens and young men are hungry.
Silence has spread to every part of every garden;
The beautiful parrots inside go hungry.
Those who always took their heads in their hands;
Those youths of the high mountains are hungry.
Those who would celebrate *Eid* with cheers,
Today, those cheerful youths are hungry.
One's tablecloth might be full of all kinds of fruits,
But all the prisoners jailed in Cuba go hungry.
O *Eid*, why do you come to this ruined village?
Those mountain slopes that would be habitable and fruitful,
They are empty now; the children are hungry.

What should I, Naseri, do with *Eid*'s happiness
On this day when my dear martyr's children are hungry?

Ustad Abdul Wali Naseri
October 4, 2008

I remember, O God!

My God! I remember the handcuffed prisoners.
I feel pain in my heart for those who were martyred,
I am crying and tears are streaming from my eyes like rain.
I am waiting for them, they might come to me.
What use do I have for makeup when I see crying everywhere.
I feel sad, sad, even though it is *Eid*, *Eid*;
They are walking in groups, laughing in the bazaar.
I feel sad when I remember the orphans;
When will certainty and confidence come to my heart?
O God! Release Hamza from piles of grief,
Release me from grief and give me happiness.

Mohammad Ismael Hamza

Eid

Eid came, but I am waiting for another *Eid*.
The beloved came, but I am waiting for another beloved.
O my poor homeland! What calamities did you not see?
Doomsday came, but I am waiting for another doomsday.

Sharafuddin Azimi
October 1, 2008

Ulemaa'

For those who draw close to a group during their life,
God will join them with that group on Doomsday.
For those who fall in love with the Talib and the *Alim*,[116]
God will praise them on Doomsday.
The *Ulemaa'* are the heirs of the prophets;
Those who love them are successful.

They are our leaders in this world;
Those who oppose them will perish.
They will be embarrassed in this world and in front of the
    religious,
He who obeys the foreigners in his activities.
The person who looks at the universe with an insult is a
    hypocrite;
He is not faithful; our prophet has testified against him.
As long as Kheywawal Mohammad Omar is alive;
He will serve the *Ulemaa'* of Deoband.

Mohammad Omar Kheywawal

Abraham's Love

My dear! Glances grow coy among your looks;
People are astonished by some of you humans.
When you appeared, love and brotherhood spread around,
O great God! The great ones are astonished by your greatness.
Not only Zuleikha wanted him, but[117]
Worlds were astonished by Joseph's charm.[118]
When he passed from the world,
The sky and earth were astonished by my beloved.
However much Nimrod tried to throw him to the fire,[119]
But by the love of Abraham, the fires were astonished.[120]
The wisdom of foreigners were shocked by his love,
Majbur! Words are astonished by your imagination.

Majbur
December 23, 2007

Hope

I seek the healing of my injured heart by the holy Lord,
I am ill and need a cure from the great doctor.
To be ready to fight the cruel,
I seek prayers for the poor widows and orphans.
I seek such charity, generosity and alms
In which there will be no insults for the poor.
A body that worships its creator with humility,
I seek such a real body and spirit.

One who would obey its parents,
I seek someone like Abraham's son.[121]
One who serves his people honestly,
I seek such a leader, such a watchman for the community.
One who respects knowledge,
I seek light for such philosophies.
Those who spend time in the darkness of prisons,
I seek freedom for them in this world.
One whose name goes higher than the galaxies,
I seek Laila's bright and fresh face.
There are many hopes in your heart, O Jamal,
I just seek my beloved's satisfaction.

Jamal

Raining Stones

Is it raining stones or not?
Do you feel my weakness or not?
From every place there is a voice saying
'Do you imagine martyrdom or not?'
The destination to which only one step remains;
Do you remember it or not?
How can I illustrate the present picture just with dots?
Has the good life stopped breathing or not?
People's looks communicated this to me:
'Do you receive my regards or not?'
He is able to make the deserts green and habitable;
Aman! Beg and pray that you may be accepted.

Aman Afridi
December 16, 2007

What's the explanation?

Tell man what the explanation for a lifetime is,
What the strong plan for your life is.
Divide the time and place and discuss each moment,
What the action and effect in each period is.
Open what was malicious and reveal the secrets of truth.
Look deeply at what the secrets are,

Look deeply at what the explanation for the secrets is.
Once you see *Allah*'s knowledge of activities,
You will for sure know the essence of destiny.
Go with the caravan, monitor it as far as its destination,
Bring the news, what is the light, what is its fate.
Open your eyes, send the pictures to your heart,
Ask vision and insight what the picture is of.
Dust is awake and alive, even if you suspect it and do not accept
   it,
Ask him what the details are.

October 25, 2008

Human

The blood of Adam's heart,
As it changed to love.

Look at the power of *Allah*;
Humans were created by him.

Time passes,
People don't know it.

Angels have brought to this world
This nice human.

Human love and humans
Were created by the Lord of the universe.

He is surprised by this world,
The grandchild of Adam, human.

June 25, 2008

Discontent

Turban

White clouds and white hills in the sky;
White, white dew had descended from there.
Sometimes, it came to our place;
It was the Kunar river's white, white duck.
This became a martyr's shroud in the Laili desert;
It was the Talib's beautiful white, white turban
That survived this attack.
The cunning enemy's palace was white, white.
The one who ousted his enemy in the past,
It was Maiwandi's white, white sword.
The one who woke youths up with *tapis*,[122]
It was zealous white, white Malalai.
The one who whitened her black hair for an orphan,
It was our Afghan white, white widow.
The one who was martyred by the crusaders,
It was Helmandi's white, white bride.
In the dawn, he from whom Janbaz sought forgiveness,
His collar was white, white from his weeping.

Janbaz

My Grave

That man would be my friend at my grave,
He who would pledge their jewellery at my grave.
They say that he died of love's fever,
For anyone who passes by my grave.
This is the sign of my martyrdom:
Birds respect my grave.
My love will be compensated.
When their black hair grows white at my grave.
Treat my grave like a small hill,
Don't spend money on my grave.
When she came on the day of *Eid* to the shrine,
She ate many fishes at my grave.
They saw Tanha's name on the tombstone,[123]
Everyone started crying at the grave.

Mujahed Tanha

Soil

All that exists will vanish.
This inexistence will again become existent.
Watch the world until Doomsday;
Some people will die.
A moment won't occur before its appointed time;
Nothing will be added to this lifetime.
Things might be added to the houses of some,
And things might be taken from the houses of others.
We were created from soil,
Everyone turns back into soil.
To those who didn't witness any damage,
How could they understand the benefit?
Congratulations on your happiness,
Your state is full of sadness.
A candle is well known because
Someone, like a moth, is burnt up in it.

Kabir Shinwari

I want a heart

I want a heart that can empathise with the discontent;
I want to be burned together with such a moth.
For a little pain and pity for sympathy,
If they exist in a heart, I want to be sacrificed for that.
Whenever I notice a pain-filled sob or a face behind a candle,
I want to cry like those who pay a visit to patients.
Hearts are cold; like a moth I seek out the fire,
I never want to stay in such a cold house.
Everyone eagerly looks at the beautiful faces;
I wish the pale faces of the poor were also watched.
I am not one to get friendly with sweet words,
But in times of sorrow and misery I want to be full of grief.
Olfat never wishes anything on anyone, but
I am looking out for my heart, not to have the red or the
    white.[124]

Gul Pacha Olfat[125]
December 16, 2007

I became a beggar, poor

I became a beggar, poor;
You became popular, and then a prince.
I became a wanderer and a vagrant;
You started laughing and watched.
I became oppressed, then homeless;
You got ready to kill me.
No problem, these situations will pass;
You became a memory in my life.

Bismillah Wardak
August 22, 2008

New Era

In this era of Yazid, I am respectable.[126]
May God bless us in this vicious era.
The conscience of my imagination was created free,
How can I be a slave in this doubtful era?
The era of extreme cruelty of friends,
The Kabul of my heart was martyred in this era.
There are the uproars of living along with
Any development in this era.
The eyes of my heart are not tired;
They will be able to see through the dark night.
In this era, Haidar always criticises
The justice and rights of oppressed people.

Sher Mohammad Haidar
December 23, 2007

Empty Shell

I thought it was an eagle but it turned out to be a crow.
Man wasn't made from him, and turned out neutral.
I trained him with the love of my heart;
I wanted to make a heart out of him, but he came out like lungs.
I held him with a great weight among the community;
He turned out just as light as a pack of straw.
He toyed with the jihadi resolve;

But it seems he turned out like the Russians.
He dances for US dollars,
We have said his fortune turned out sinister.
Khalis does not complain from anyone else;
The bullet in his own pocket turned out to be just an empty
    shell.

Mawlawi Yunis Khalis
October 28, 2008

Everybody said 'that's me'

When there was no examining, everybody would say, 'that's me'.
When the exam came, I only said, 'that's me'.
When I handed out money, my uncle said, 'that's me'.
My elder brother said, 'that's me' and my friend said, 'that's me'.
Both young and old were coming with sincerity;
The children would say, 'but that's me', and the old would say,
    'that's me'.
It was too crowded and was a public competition,
Everybody would repeatedly say, 'that's me'.
They were ready for a position in the Emirate and for leadership;
The animal-like human with a large belly said, 'that's me'.
Each one of them was able to bear the problem of eating,
Every one seriously said, 'that's me'.
Suddenly, when the test appeared,
The zeal of a friend required said, 'that's me'.

Abdullah
August 8, 2008

Ghazal

He would say all kinds of things, my desire was crazy,
Alas! My tongue is numb to pain and emotion.

Our path in life is the one full of thorns,
From the pain, each alas of ours, each breath of ours is a sigh.

Greetings to the Highness! Perhaps our mouths are opened to
   complain about
the pairing of everyone else, our world is demolished.

God knows when they will reach their fate;
The bride of wishes is sitting in the palanquin of our hearts.

On the nose of whose martyr it maybe was hanging;
Today it is thrown away in the dust.

Iqbal! Don't lose yourself, still time remains;
Your *ghazal* has not changed into a rose, still it is a blossom.

Iqbal
January 16, 2007

Ghazal

Again the uproars of love have begun;
The teller of tales is worried.
Fate! Again you passed me over for grief;
Convoys have started to proceed to the land of friendship.
Cheeks turn pale and we are frightened;
The enemy of God comes under attack.
Before, mosques were places for worship,
Now, other strange deeds are carried out there.
Mansour! Well done! Be a little bit more daring;
Deflating that, the distances have started to decrease.

Mansour Khatak
December 16, 2007

Interior Garments

Nothing tastes good for the sick,
But when they recover, they taste everything.
Decorate your interior garments,
Patch up your exterior appearance.
Reputation and bravery don't come from clothes;
It should be either the hero of Panipat or Maiwand.[127]
Hardships will reoccur for those who

110

Have not learnt from history.
Virtue comes from effort;
It can't be obtained just by sitting at home.
He will be capable of greatness and leadership,
He who has devoted his life to service.
Privilege and manliness is due to merit,
It's not just that you are a Ghilzai or Mohmand.[128]
Arrogance takes away from honour and esteem,
Patience and modesty increase them many times.
O friendly dust, who is living in the palace of wealth,
The place where you lay your head in expectation.

October 25, 2008

Unfaithful World

It passed, is passing and will pass this world;
It passed for both the king and for the beggar.
This transitory world passes; some are happy about that and
    some unhappy;
The more one has, the more one forgets.
They can take nothing with them and with empty hands they will
    proceed to the grave;
Neither power nor crown will offer any help at that time.
Worlds ended, are ending and will end;
This is responsibility; you are not to forget it.
This is wrong: it doesn't match Islam;
Watanwal Dawlat says O lion! You will turn into a fox!

Watanwal
December 16, 2007

The Language of the Nightingale

In this garden, each bud has lost control;
The tongue of the nightingale is aflame, it halts the uproar.
It can't applaud, grief has sapped its strength;
The sister can't sing melodies for the brother's wedding party.
Let's sing a song together, my dear:
Why is our life so pale and poor?
O flower! Each branch of my life

111

Has been rescued from the sickle of your eyelashes.
Buildings of brotherhood have now become ruins;
Now, brotherly relations with a brother from the same parents
can't even be sustained.
Black hearts will no longer be interested in the black of your
eyes;
Now, I am not one to discriminate between black and white.
Oh friends! I, Andaleeb, am not crying about flowers for no
reason:
Constantly, many funerals were held at my thorny house.

Andaleeb
December 23, 2007

Poetic Competition

I beseech you, O appreciative poet,
Always write the truth, O poet.
In writing what is right, don't care about anyone else;
You are the consummate translator of the Muslim *Umma*, O
poet.
God has conferred great power to your pen,
Unite the Muslims with your pen, O poet.
Never write for your reputation, O writer,
Yours is the tongue of the nation and its eyes as well, O poet.
You will be questioned for each word you write;
Don't write things that you'll regret in the future.
Leave the Godar, Mangai, black ringlet and eyes as well;[129]
Cry for the sorrow of the homeland; leave the *pizwan*, O poet.[130]
Do *jihad* with your pen; that is your obligation today;
Fight cruelty on every battlefield, O poet.
I, Kheywawal Omar, am asking for God's kindness;
Go spread the word and make your faith, O poet.

 Mohammad Omar Kheywawal

Thin Tongue

Your pen holds the power of positive change;
It contains love and charm for hearts.
Hard hearts are melted by its tears;
It has many effects and blessings.
Pious God has granted it great respect;
Its thin tongue holds much virtue and achievement.
It doesn't act as if white is black and black is white;
Because finally that ends in awful embarrassment.
Write what is real and take the right path;
You will be helped and blessed by God.
Write each line as a prescription for the pains of the country;
If you desire honour, there is honour in this affair.
Oh Zeerak! Telling the truth is considered to be *jihad*;
Martyrdom is granted to he who dies for what is true.

Zeerak

Pity

Tongues cannot speak the truth;
Mouths cannot allow the voice of truth to emerge.
Justice is not present for us to hear the voices of the martyrs;
Omar isn't here to distinguish between right and wrong.[131]
Osman – who had collated the *Qur'an* – isn't here;
Ali – who captured the Khyber – isn't here.
Those who would always sacrifice themselves for religion are
    gone.
Who will open their mouths now, for God's sake?
In the past, Muslims were leading all men.

* *

The kebab rained down tears,
The coal's fire got hotter.
Count the Pharaoh of the time like this as well;
As you cry down on them, their fire becomes more serious.

Abdul Azim
May 22, 2008

Neck

Sometimes better people are found and they end what is bad;
Think about both of them for a while.
The doors to fortune are open to you,
Don't tie a rope around your neck.
There are always many jewels in the river,
You won't get anything by sticking to the sides.
There is everything for you in this city,
Don't walk uselessly among the ruins.
Come out and see the big universe,
You can't stay in a hole like a worm.
Hunt fresh prey for yourself, like a lion;
There is no esteem for you in being dirty.
Take up your pen and go down the path of existence,
You can't reach anywhere if you just stop at one place.
Go and beautify the red blood,
There are more flavours in its water than just honey.

Badar Bakhari

Value

How could they know the value of your beauty's springs?
Paths turned to thorns, how would they know the value of
    wounds?
He arrives like a wayfarer and makes his way back;
Time is faithless, how would it know the value of lifetimes?
May I be sacrificed to your Farhadi reliance, O Muslim;[132]
Nobody knows the value of your black, black mountains.
Neither Rahman nor zealous Khushal will return;[133]
How could the enemies know the value of our celebrations?
When you get the chance, visit your beloved;
How else could the unwise know the value of visiting?
Yesterday when I dreamed of my former competitor,
Similar to separation, how could he know the value of burnt
    hearts?
Karwan isn't complimenting flowerlike faces;
How could this ignorant person know the value of *ghazals*?[134]

Noor Ali Karwan

114

Standing Confused

O Afghan maiden! Let me ask you something:
I am proud of your beauty.
For the sake of *Allah*, walk modestly;
I pity your condition.
Your brave brothers have gone to the wars;
They departed out of grief for their sick homeland.
They left when they heard stories of the poor life;
Why are you unaware of yourself?
You are not a traveller in your own homeland;
You changed your own clothes to a western style.
Everyone looks at you;
You put on makeup when you leave home.
You go to the bazaar and have fun.
Other issues don't come to mind;
Why do you do these things?
You are the daughter of Malalai;
Why don't your eyes feel shame?
I am standing confused. My God, what should I do?
Your Naseri is crying out of sadness.

Alam Gul Naseri

Malalai's Wish

May my beloved get lost, because loyalty can't be expected of
    him;
Beauty is everywhere, but beauty isn't expected of them.
It seems that the nightingale's feelings have been hurt by
    someone;
He walks on the lawn but laughter isn't expected of him.
If this isn't the power of Western colonialism, then what is?
Women walk around naked, modesty isn't expected of them.
What complaint can my sister Malalai have?
She sat with her *hijab*, dancing isn't expected of her.[135]
There are many eloquent mouths in the world,
They are mute because the correct words aren't expected of
    them.
All people have eyes, but they don't bear tears;
May they get lost, because crying isn't expected of them.

There may be many Muslims on paper;
They want depravity, and goodness isn't expected of them.

Mohammadi

Ghazal

I keep the arrows of expectation in my heart like flowers;
My friend, I keep the lamp of hope lit for your coming.
I incite many lovers' hearts to dance to the sound of my voice;
Always, like the nightingale, I keep the melody of grief in my
    heart.
Yet it is too young to be hurt; I am afraid it may hurt itself;
I will certainly safeguard this loin from the forest.
Even if time brings the ugliest revolutions,
I will keep the fold of my turban pious.
Sayyed! Even if I am destined to live in far away cities,
I will remain the rough Pashtun of the mountains.

Sayyed
December 4, 2007

Impostor

He made happy unhappy and unhappy happy,[136]
The impostor has come, he is blind.
He says that he is God, claiming he brought someone back to
    life;
When he expressed his inner self, I was astonished.
He deemed what is *halal* as *haram* and *haram* as *halal*.
The impostor has come, he is blind.
Driving in a car he speaks out in a different direction,
It is called a mobile; the telephone's a strange device.
Obviously it works, but its corruptions are inside,
It has turned beautiful to ugly and ugly to beautiful.
The impostor has come, he is blind.[137]

Wahhaj
December 16, 2007

116

What I See

I see around the world how some people make the *ka'aba* and
    some make statues;
False knowledge turns humans to devils.
Good manners, neatness and good clothes are necessary;
If "fashion" increases, the youths will all become dancers.
Not everyone is expected to make the land flourish;
Architects build good houses from mud and stones.
If human lightness registers in someone's brain,
He will try to become a real human in this world.
There are many differences among humans in their conception;
All are busy; some people make themselves, some make the
    world.

Gul Pacha Olfat
December 23, 2007

Quatrains

Some turn themselves around,
Some go round their beloved.
The people I desire are those
Who care about the entire world.

* *

If you count the heads, there are many;
Men with little fight are uncountable.
But count those men among men
Who offer their lives for others.

* *

The world today is better than yesterday,
Tomorrow will be better than today.
Alas, Afghans don't know how to go forward;
They are slipping backwards into dust.

Kamal
May 14, 2008

117

Condolences of Karzai and Bush

Karzai:
O hello, my lord Bush;
Now that you've gone, who did you leave me with?

Bush:
My slave, dear Karzai!
Don't be upset; I am handing you over to Obama.

Karzai:
These words make me happy.
Tell me, how long will I be here?

Bush:
Karzai! Wait for a year;
Don't come till I send someone else there.

Karzai:
Life is tough without you my darling;
I share in your grief; I am coming to you.

Bush:
As for death, we'll both die;
Alas, we'll be first and next.

Karzai:
Give me your hand as you go;
Turn your face as you disappear.

Bush:
Sorrow takes over and overwhelms me;
My darling! Take care of yourself and I will take care of myself.

Karzai:
Mountains separate you from me;
Say hello to the pale moon and I'll do so as well.

December 18, 2008

Slave

Karzai! You sold the country for a few dollars.
As you are a wrong-doer, to whom should we complain?
In our beloved country, you spread adultery and wine-drinking;
Karzai! Really, you hammered the heirs of prophets;
Jews and Christians have come to this dear country of saints.
Karzai! At every moment the Prophet seems upset;
You jailed many religious scholars in Cuba's Bay[138]
Karzai! They are treated cruelly there.
When Danesh observes such cruelties
Karzai! Everyday he hopes for death while he prays.

Danesh
December 16, 2007

How long?

How long will people wander in disappointment?
How long will they wander thirsty, hungry and insecure in the
    deserts?
Most people are jobless, wandering around.
How long? You wander hungrily in deserts.
The wrecked economy deprives you of education.
How long? You pass the time waiting patiently.
Pretending to carry out reconstruction; they established personal
    businesses,
They enjoy life, and you? How long will you wander in the
    rubbish heap?
They voice hollow slogans of equality;
The salaries of a hundred men are given to one; how long will
    the poor wander?
They observe well what is going on with the oppressed people;
How long will you wander unauthorised?
Every day, our nation suffers from the fire of the enemy,
How long will the shameless puppets walk without being taken
    to account?
M.A. is astounded by such a life;
How long will they stay drunk and happy?

M.A.
December 16, 2007

Afghanistan

The wish in the depths of my heart:
That wish of mine remembers Afghans,
That our collapsed turbans rise up once again,
That poor society remembers the godly people,
That this republic system will be built,
That each individual of this nation remembers the mystics,
That the good fortune of the new generation is a given,
Because they recall a properly-built Afghanistan.
These are the poems of Armani;
He mentions the elders in his *ghazal.*

Mohammad Wali Armani

My Cottage

O homeland of beauty, be well!
May your flag be raised all over the world.
You have mountains,
You have full seas.
You have beautiful deserts,
You are a piece of paradise; be this paradise!
O homeland of beauty, be well!
You are the trench of the brave.
You are the rug of the Pashtuns,
You are the liver of every Afghan.
You are my cottage; be honourable;
O homeland of beauty, be well!
You are the turban of honour,
You are our respite amidst a long walk.
May your enemy be blamed everywhere,
O homeland of beauty, be well!

August 18, 2008

My Homeland

The land of the brave and of heroes,
The land of Malalai and Nazo.[139]
The depths of the high Pamir became full again

With your love stories, my homeland!
Once again, it's an eaglet flying
On the peaks of the high mountains.
We'll sacrifice ourselves to you,
My homeland of the partridge-eyed and those with the green
  mark.[140]
May you be honoured amongst your competitors,
Land of turbans.
Once again, make the leaves garden green,
The land of pines and cypresses.

Noor Mohammad Saeed
September 15, 2008

Our Life, O Afghanistan

May independence return to you once more,
May each of your feet be flowers.

Our spirit, our body!
Our life, O Afghanistan!

We have been born in your lap,
We have grown up and trained as well.

We would save you with our firm faith,
Our spirit, our body!

Our life, O Afghanistan!

Whether we are spread out to the west or to the east,
Our country is the same and we are from the same stock.

You are the honour of all Afghans
Our spirit, our body!

Our life, O Afghanistan!

We may be at any corner of the world,
But we sacrifice ourselves for your name.

We would raise your name to the sky,
Our spirit, our body!

Our life, O Afghanistan!

You will again find heroes like Aman[141]
You will again find lions like Akbar[142]

You are the homeland of Afghans.

Our spirit, our body!
Our life, O Afghanistan!

Mustafa Hamid
September 4, 2008

Prayer

Turn all our girls into Malalai and all our boys into Ghaznawi![143]
Make every stone marble and make every flower pink!
For those Afghan brothers who left because they were poor,
Bring them back to the homeland and end their emigration.
Whether they are in the East or in the West, they are all Afghans;
O God! Unite them and bring brotherhood amongst them.
Whether Pashtun, Uzbek, Hazara or Tajik,
They are all one Afghan nation; may you end their enmity.
This is the cry of Majbur's heart; hear it!
And to those who want bad things for Afghans, may they go
    mad!

Qudratullah Majbur
May 30, 2008

Homeland Song

I want to honour my homeland, no matter if I am hanged,
I shall sacrifice to you, my homeland.
If someone beheads me for you,
If I am cut into pieces,
I will be proud as if I were your servant.
I will never obey anyone else as long as I live.

I will never bow down to anyone.
I don't accept to obey foreigners.
I took the zeal from my mother's milk,
I took some lessons from my father.
I shall not step aside,
I don't desire power or a crown.
I desire nothing but you.
I don't care about being burned.
Death to he who is treacherous to you!
I never wanted happiness for them: I want them to be upset.
I shall be out of reach of those people,
I don't call him a Pashtun when he becomes a slave.
I don't bear the problems of those who salute to the foreigners,
I don't allow them;
Rich Watanwal would rather be poor.
Better to pain my heart for you;
I've never claimed to be a master.

Watanwal
December 16, 2007

Why are we separated?

We are all descended from Afghans, so why are we separated?
Whose cruelties cause us to scream out?
Our women wander around each corner;
Why do we – cowardly youths – laugh at that?
Some were lost in Iran, some in Pakistan,
When will we gather together?
The reason: our country is divided into four parts.
For our faults this is why we Pashtuns speak Dari.
Today, Sahar does not allow us to be calm;
Because we are living in accordance with our religious principles.

Sahar
December 16, 2007

Culture

O time! Don't eliminate our culture,
Don't destroy our traditions.

Don't burn us up, for we are voicing our rights;
O time! Don't eliminate our feelings and our consciousness.
We'll grant we believe in insanity and in love with any ruthless
    amusement;
Don't extinguish our excitement.
Don't blame us for the barriers of dignity on paths and ways;
We are hungover from the wine of bravery.
People say that Afghans have an uncouth appearance;
Don't strike us down for this fault, for our characters.
We are simple, we've not learnt a life of deception;
Don't eliminate us for our enemies.
Each moment he dies with the poison of poverty;
Don't eliminate this poor hard-working servant.
Poverty has killed him many times;
Don't kill someone as needy as Erfaan.

Erfaan
December 23, 2007

Poetic Speech

My God, what misfortune has fallen upon our homeland?
There is widespread robbery and wine-soaked "freedom".
There is disobedience of God and disrespect for the Prophet;
This is a life of ill-repute and misfortune.
We are the slaves of foreigners inside our own homeland;
Everywhere people think only about themselves; friendships are
    made with Satan.
There is a distance between hearts, and friendships with
    unbelievers;
There is luxury: what a strange republic this is!
There is insecurity: what a strange democracy this is!
Human worships human and the awkward activities of unworthy
    people are going on.
The infidels are bombing the poor from every side;
Who is doing the spying for this to happen? There is disrespect
    of the *Qur'an*.
There is the fluttering of dollars, slavery of the infidels;
There is our poverty, and friendship to the Western countries.
They are cheating us and calling it human love; there is a plot
    against our religion;
Whether they be Pashtun or Tajik, Hanafism is our religion.[144]

Our nation is Abrahamic, and against idolatry;
For those who are slaves, there is a defect in their faith.
This scream comes from every oppressed mouth,
Whether it's London, America, Denmark or Canada,
Whether it's Russia, France, the Netherlands or Britain;
This is Mikhaeel's cry; may they all be disgraced around the
world.

Mikhaeel
September 1, 2008

Freedom

Every single breath of life requires freedom;
Freedom is the great gift of *Allah*.
Freedom is the beginning of a strong determination;
It is the name of honour, the name of the sword and the name of
bravery.
Freedom is a holy word;
Reaching it needs a million heads.
Freedom in every step requires
The swords' blow and the roar of the lions.
Freedom has songs buried in its breast,
It has melodies, it has beauty and love.
In which even afflicted hearts dance,
It has colourful days, nights and moments.
Freedom is like the fourteen-day moon,
It is like the silence of your beloved's bosom.
Why would the community deal with hate, then?
When will there be freedom of conscience?
Freedom is the honourable veil of the nations;
Its price is uncountable.
Freedom is like tears of happiness,
Where even the heart forgets the reason for their arrival.
Freedom is the natural right of every human;
They should live with love beside each other.

Mohammad Sabir Khan Bereya
September 23, 2008

Wound

It seems to me that everything has changed,
It seems there is deception amidst our friendship.
I had gone with you sincerely
But your footsteps show you have taken the wrong path.
I don't trust your admissions anymore,
Full of frauds, it seems you are a thief of the tamarisks.
Here, lamps are put out, darkness spreads;
Lamps are turned on in each of your houses.
Saqi! I desire intoxication, but don't bring me more wine;[145]
Your bottle is the murderer of love.
It walks on much thinner paths;
Your end seems to have arrived.
I am not incredulous, I know it all too well;
The sky seems to be the core of the earth.
Latun has inflicted many gashes on the heart;
Every *Ghazal* is painful.

Luftullah Latun Tokhi
December 16, 2007

On the occasion of the 89th Anniversary of the British Occupation

May I take up the troubles of your stones, O my homeland,
I haven't forgotten, you are always on my mind.

I have seen many countries,
　　　I have drunk water in several places.

May the entire world be like the soil under your feet.

O my homeland,
　　　I haven't forgotten, you are always on my mind.

Mountains, valleys, beautiful deserts,
You have wavy seas,
Beautiful flowers in your deserts.

Each of your people is dear to me,
Each valley of yours is Khyber,
You beat the superpowers in every century.

O my homeland,
      I haven't forgotten, you are always on my mind.

You are my pride, you are my dignity,
You are my world's paradise.

I will sacrifice everything of mine for you.

O my homeland,
      I haven't forgotten, you are always on my mind.

Afghans in the west and in the east are all one,
Lovers of this area are all one,
They have lost their heads on the path of zeal.

O my homeland,
      I haven't forgotten, you are always on my mind.

We will either unite the west and east,
Or we'll end our lives.
These are the promises of the lions to you.

O my homeland,
      I haven't forgotten, you are always on my mind.

Your position and honour is so high,
Complimenting you is the duty of Hamidpur.
O Afghanistan, may I be sacrificed for you.

O my homeland,
      I haven't forgotten, you are always on my mind.

Hamidpur
September 4, 2008

Kabul is set on fire

A hot bazaar of cruelty is being made out of beautiful Kabul,
It is being set on fire, it has all turned to fire.
Because of the oppressions of the Pharaohs
Noises and cries are heard in the houses of the martyrs.
Everybody is experimenting on Kabul's soil,
A great power of superpowers is made.
The remnants of others are brought for us to eat,
Pir Baba's shrine is made from my home today.[146]
Nobody can tell the foreigners to stop what they're doing,
A few hired slaves are ruling the country.
O Kabul! We will clean you from these black faces,
Lines of committed believers are formed.
The signs of freedom are evident, you'll become independent,
Each Afghan's honour is in jeopardy.
They are waiting that they might bring freedom again,
Muslims' hopes have risen for such an army.
Everyone is invited to the trench,
Every fighter is now Hafiz Haqyar.

Hafiz Ikramuddin
August 8, 2008

Food

The food of the big snakes of the time,
Our blood is the food of the wolves.
Those who came received it for free;
The food of the cruel governors.
They don't count it when they eat our blood;
They think there is no death; the food of the rich.
This is blood that can brook no alternative;
They always become the food of the *Ghazis*.[147] *Islamic warrior*
In the fight between the fighters of the East and West
Our blood has become the food of the bombs.
There is no sympathy for our pains;
Some became the food of the foreigners and some the food of
    the elders.
At each moment the food of the traitors,
Around the dragon of this century,

Is the the blood of this poor nation;
The food of the traders of the bazaar.
In the name of peace and reconciliation,
Our bodies and property have become the food of the cheaters.
When will the killers of Sangaryar's wishes
Become the food of the scorpions.

Sifatullah Sangaryar

How many are the NGOs!

Wasting time, they merely sit in their offices,
How many are the NGOs!
Their salaries, more than ministers',
How many are the NGOs!
Wasting time, respecting recommendations,
Those who have no recommendations are forgotten.
How many are the NGOs!
When you are interviewed, they ask for recommendations.
During interviews they make tension suddenly;
How many are the NGOs!
When there is a vacancy, boys are appointed;
They will not admit that they are over-aged,
How many are the NGOs!
If the applicants are girls, they will be admitted without
interview;
Women in large numbers but men are few.
How many are the NGOs!
Most people who broke with the government move to NGOs;
The reason is, salaries are in dollars,
How many are the NGOs!
People come from here and there taking salaries in dollars;
They don't work in the government because they have their
hearts broken,
How many are the NGOs!
If someone gets to be head of an NGO, then he is rich,
So they enjoy a better living situation than Karzai.
How many are the NGOs!
Perform the tricks, spend large amounts;
It is not clear where these people come from;
How many are the NGOs!

A meddler strolls around with his bodyguards;
That Afghan doesn't think about the situation;
How many are the NGOs!

Matiullah Sarachawal
December 23, 2007

Justice

Those who are madly in love are mostly hit by stones;
A mountain will never move if it is hit by stones.
O God! Bless us, what grief will come to me next?
They hit the door of my heart with their looks.
It is not wise; they take me to the faithless.
Let them, if they hit my head with stones.
Where did humanity leave the world?
Look at the human who hits the other human.
For a visit, if we climb up to its shrine,
These silly people will then hit the sun with stones.
Oh Tawab! I am astonished by this justice!
When their work is done they hit the labourers with stones.

Tawab Turabi
December 23, 2007

Couplets

From one side the enemies of our homeland create problems for
     us,
From the other the black-faced bearers of tales cause trouble.
O God! Scatter the enemies of this land!
What did we do wrong? They don't leave us alone.

* *

I had a friend staying near the high mountains that I lost;
Not before, but recently I lost him.
Everyone mourns in the house of my martyred friend;
O God! Have pity on me, I lost him in a tumult.

* *

If only there were a world with a peaceful life;
I wish weapons were done away with and machines made from
  them.
I wish there was affection among people's hearts and that nations
  were brothers;
I wish humans were valued and would wishing each other
  goodness.

****

Where were you yesterday? There was a strong earthquake;
We fell under sorrow and an affront of pain.
We were trapped in difficulties from the top to the bottom;
The sky was clear and bright, but we passed a dark day.

December 16, 2007

Anxiety

Just like the dew-damaged thin rose petals,
The rubab's strings have damaged my fingertips.[148]

O messenger of separation! You can never be forgiven;
You ruined the red-lipped smiles of youth.

You who have been hitting the cup with stones,
It appears that somebody else's good deeds made up for your
  sins.

Our love and blood both share the same story;
Someone has ruined the few golden lines of our book.

Abaceen's shores have been deserted, O border Pashtun;
Which cursed person damaged the leaves of your green trees?

The bangles of beautiful women were broken in Torkham with
  sticks;
The lives of many teenage women have come to ruin in the jails
  of Punjab.

Remember! I will not forget this, O black-legged friend;
You had the big butcher eat our flesh.

131

Your poems are mute; your voice is lost, O Mutma'in;
It seems that you, too, have been affected by anxiety about the
    current situation

Abdul Hai Mutma'in

Cruel Oppressor

This is he who doesn't keep his promises and is unfaithful;
This is he who is familiar with everyone.
This is he for whom my life is written together, as destiny;
This is he who is an oppressor.
I am the nightingale of the red flowers;
This is he, a beautiful bloom of the desert.
How much my own tears have dampened my collar;
This is my beloved who isn't afraid of God.
Abdullah Shabiwal is tired of life;
This is he who sacrifices himself for love.

Abdullah Shabiwal

I tell this to Bush!

Bush! Don't get upset, just listen to a few words.

Listen to my bittersweet words!
You are neither God nor can the light of God be discerned in
    your face.
My Shamshad looks like a small mount Sinai.
There is no Pharaoh now, but you made a Pharaoh of yourself.
Every human in this world now looks like an enemy to you
With whose blood you relieved your thirst again.
A red dagger appears to be in your hand again.

Bush! Don't get upset, just listen to a few words.

You climbed to the roof again; who you are monitoring?
Which village you are going to bomb with red bullets?
All those who you killed will grab your collar.
How can you deny their deaths?

Bush! Don't get upset, just listen to a few words.

You kill the young so that their maidens will cry in Iraq again,
May you be killed so that your children will cry for you.
May your mother, sister and grandmother cry for you,
You devote your life to the killing of innocents.
You came here and gave our way to strangers,
Who knows why you gave it to the foreigners.
What kind of friendship have you started with us?
We are Afghans, but you gave our soil to the foreigners.
You struck the mountains and throw bombs at them,
You cut the pines from them and gave the snow upon them to
    the foreigners.

Bush! Don't get upset, just listen to a few words.

You have become crazy, you are looking for life in the graves.
You came out of the nice city of lights.
You are seeking your life in our black walls.
You are taking advantage of the poor.
You are seeking your life in their hearts for a few dollars.

Bush! Don't get upset, just listen to a few words.

Ezatullah Zawab
August 23, 2008

Cruel Man

He's not a Mullah, he left his pulpit;[149]
He isn't clever, his leader left him.
O cruel man! Don't be so harsh
That you didn't leave him either in the city or the mountains.
In this wealthy homeland of my father,
You didn't leave any rubies or jewellery.
From this troubled and tortured nation,
You didn't leave the young or the adults.
In your cruel and inaccurate bombing
You didn't spare any village or tribe.
O Kabul, this Yazidi army[150]
Didn't spare your wounded chest.

O Hoshmand, if you speak these true words,
Be aware that you are endangering your life.

Najibullah Hoshmand
May 27, 2008

Voice of Peace

May you be lost from the world and fall into the trap of tricks,
He who parts from the group may fall from the peaks.
The enemy is either native or a foreigner; he is a duplicitous
    friend.
May the calamity of time fall on this type of native and foreigner.
This cruel decision of time or an enemy,
Afghans fall in the villages of the East and the West.
Should I complain about my luck or the sky
Because the youths fall due to the provocations of others?
Many took this wish to the grave,
Seeing Pashtun flowers fall from the turbans.
I will break the spine of the competitors whether they are Afghan
    or foreign
If the struggles and disputes of Afghans come to an end.
Matin's heart is pounding with wishes;
The voice of our homeland's peace falls on the valleys.

Engineer Matin

War Talk

Don't talk of cheeks and beauty here any more;
Pack up your words about make-up and beauty.
Now is not the time for complimenting pots and springs;[151]
Let's talk about the blows of white swords.
The old songs are very old now;
Now, remember the words for the clink of the handcuffs.
Don't remind us of *Atan*s and picnics;[152]
The word for war's pollution are spoken at every opportunity.
Why do you make yourself more illegitimate?
Why are the words for turbans lost now?
Whose voice would reach from Spin Ghar to Delhi?[153]
Give the words of that powerful father back to your sons.[154]

The history of epics is not lost, reopen it!
Use words about the Tatars and the Moghuls.
You celebrate independence day so why don't you talk about
The foreigners' control of our native soil?
The fact that their foreign forces came to my homeland?
Heavy words lie on this path.
For God's sake, O Afghans and fellow Pashtuns,
Talk a little about the Western colonisation,
About what's going on with my poor nation in my homeland,
About the words of bombardment against our innocent women.
May this emotionless pen be broken and lost,
The one that still talks about love and the beloved.
If the homeland is crying, people are crying and wounds are
    crying;
O Zakir, don't you hear the words of pain and injuries?

Zakir
September 8, 2008

Zealous Head

May I be sacrificed for the head that is zealous,
One that is higher than other heads in the field.
May I be sacrificed for a head that is sacrificed for honour,
History will compliment it in the parade of the famous.
May I be sacrificed at the flag of his grave, since he safeguarded
    honour with his blood;
He'll raise the green banner among the flags of the world.
Malalai's steps compliment the head of honour and zeal,
He'll bring Ayyub's name amongst other names.[155]
That's not counting a head, but the bones of the dead who
Bow to any ignoble person for money.
I'll make the soil under his feet into the beauty of my eyes,
He who is sacrificed for the problems of the nation.
There is competition over power between black and white;
Stand up foolish one, don't be deaf. There is regret in sleep.
The zealous went to the soil but shame is for us
As we draw the murderers of the martyrs to our bosoms.
Many humans have gone from the world into the depths of the
    earth;
They are dead and there is no name for them; some are
    mentioned in history.

This is the beginning of the land; tread carefully;
Once you are incapacitated it's irreversible.
Don't make headaches for yourself, O Qatin!
Saying the truth is bitter, people are held captive by money.

Qatin
August 8, 2008

Fortress Joy

I am stuck in amongst a bundle of dollars;
Me the silly one, dealt both my life and dignity.
My homeland! You know me but I am trapped in the dollar's joy,
In a strange period of slavery.
Sometimes satisfied, sometimes hungry,
Foreigners asked me to become a slave.
I am up and sometimes down in the era of the dollar;
I run to any fortress with bravery;
I am such a soldier among the Afghans.
I, Mukhlis, remain in fortresses;
This is what I am, like a sword waiting patiently.

Zahid ul-Rahman Mukhlis
December 16, 2007

Change

A strange uproar rose up in my body,
When your emotional song reached my ears.
It was magic in words and magic in song,
It became the host of my imagination and motive of my mind.
As its voice of conscience fell in my heart,
The light of hope glimmers in an atmosphere of disappointment.
There were the blows of Ayyub Khan and the heroic poems of
    Malalai,
The story of Maiwand came to mind.
My God! There were foreign invaders in this country;
We have been changed and this is a time full of crimes.

Stanizi
August 3, 2008

The Trench

A Mujahed's Wish From His Mother

Mother! Pray for me, I am going into battle tomorrow;
I am going for *Allah*'s satisfaction, without delay;
Battle has many rewards;
Allah will grant me paradise;
If I am martyred, I'll go to my leader with a white face;
If I head to my trench
To fight against the invader,
I like pride, and will head into the afterlife with pride.
If I don't make it back home,
This is my last will to my father and mother:
Don't be impatient; I head towards doomsday with a red shroud
Until the homeland becomes free
When all the betrayers are suppressed.
I go to the punishing plains of war with great courage;
You became *Allah*'s blessing for us;
Now, we all accept you, Abu Fazl;
I'll ascend to the sky in great honour.

Abu Fazl
January 29, 2009

Goodbye

Allow me to go and to say goodbye to you,
Dear mother! I won't stay anymore, goodbye.
Englishmen have occupied my home,
By no means, I cannot stay anymore.
They play with our dignity and chastity,
I shy with my conscience.
It would be better at this moment to go to fight.

Alam Gul Naseri
July 25, 2007

I am an Afghan Mujahed

Gun in my hand and dagger under my arm, I am going to battle;
I am an Afghan *mujahed*, I am an Afghan *mujahed*.[156]
I may be a victim for my homeland a hundred times;

I am an Afghan *mujahed*, I am an Afghan *mujahed*.
I have my religion; I have my faith and the law of the holy
    Qur'an;
I am an Afghan *mujahed*, I am an Afghan *mujahed*.
Anyone who looks the wrong way at me will find himself lost for
    ever,
Look, I am a known champion in history,
I am an Afghan *mujahed*, I am an Afghan *mujahed*.
We have the proper *shari'a* and believe in it at all times,[157]
Shari'a is my light and I am light of heart in its light,
I am an Afghan *mujahed*, I am an Afghan *mujahed*.
We want a free life, we want stability for every place,
Because I love truth and will never tolerate injustice:
I am an Afghan *mujahed*, I am an Afghan *mujahed*.
We hate the war, but we are fighting in the war.
If war is imposed on us, then I am the man of the field,
I am an Afghan *mujahed*, I am an Afghan *mujahed*.
Oh cruel coloniser! Take it from me, Qatin,
I avenge the people, I am committed to my promise:
I am an Afghan *mujahed*, I am an Afghan *mujahed*.

Qatin
October 28, 2008[158]

Hero

A test is not needed,
  I am Afghan I am Afghan
History attests that
  I am a hero I am a hero
I am merciful,
  but not to the cruel
To he who attacks me,
  I am a storm I am a storm
I dedicate my life to my homeland,
  I can't accept enslavement
I am only the slave of *Allah*,
  I am a Muslim I am a Muslim
Within the movement of the times,
  I've lost my way
Muslims are oppressed,
  I am sad I am sad

What will happen when
they follow the foreigners?
I am the offspring of Afghans,
I am Mirwais Khan I am Mirwais Khan[159]
If Afghans come together
and revive the old history
I am Omar;
this has been my wish for a long time.

Omar
December 16, 2007

We are the Soldiers of Islam

We are the soldiers of Islam and we are happy to be martyred;
We are the men of the battlefield and we fight on the front lines.

We defend our religion, if we are struck for that we smile;
We appeal for liberty for our lives, we never give up.
We are the soldiers of Islam and we are happy to be martyred;
We are the men of the battlefield and we fight on the front lines.

We will eradicate all the Christians, this is our undertaking;
We depend on God, not on tools and equipment.
We are the soldiers of Islam and we are happy to be martyred;
We are the men of the battlefield and we fight on the front lines.

We are the heroes of the era and we are the conquerors of every
    field;
Our enemies are shivering, we mount their forts.
We are the soldiers of Islam and we are happy to be martyred;
We are the men of the battlefield and we fight on the front lines.

Once again the Khan of this era – like Ayyub Khan was the
    conqueror –
We will remind them of Maiwand and we will reach Washington
We are the soldiers of Islam and we are happy to be martyred;
We are the men of the battlefield and we fight on the front lines.

Those who are imprisoned in corridors and under the Israeli
    hawks
Are looking at the prelude of a rising flood; we will not be
    deceived by their patrols and watchmen.
We are the soldiers of Islam and we are happy to be martyred;
We are the men of the battlefield and we fight on the front lines.

Oh Muslims! Rise up! And March towards the *qibla* of Sutton[160]
I am Ramani, advising you to get ready; we will reach our goal.

Ramani
January 1, 2007

Strong-willed

Don't raise your head;
    I am strong-willed.
Cruel man! Don't spread your dollars around,
    I have a revolutionary religion.
You'd best be leaving now,
    I have sons born of Malalai.
Just ask the British,
    I have an army like Akbar Khan.
Just ask the Russians,
    I can tell you tales of war.
I made the Russians kneel;
    I have daring youths.
I will sacrifice myself
    for I have the *shari'a* of Mohammad.
Jihad is my path ahead
    and I will be proud to be sacrificed.
What does the world matter?
    I have Mohammad as my leader.
I devote my life to my religion;
    I long for the day of judgement.

Khan Alim Mujahed
December 16, 2007

Ghazal

O Afghans! Be a little daring;
Take a little power and love each other.
Look! You do everything to Britain;
Become a bit more Pashtun and dignified.
They insult our women;
Be a little bit more daring and learn some humanity.
We will get higher ranks when
We become courageous and practice justice.
I, Ahaahyar Ibrahim say:
Be zealous like our ancestors!

Ibrahimi
December 16, 2007

O sons of the brave! Be careful not to be confused

O sons of the brave! Be careful not to be confused;
Go forward step by step, be careful not to move backwards.

This is the land of Muslims,
    this is the land of great Afghans.
This has the mark of paradise,
    this is the land of the holy *Qur'an*.

O sons of the brave! Be careful not to be confused;
Go forward step by step, be careful not to move backwards.

Plots are being made against you,
    many conspiracies as well.
Scenarios against you,
    Different types of tricks as well.

O sons of the brave! Be careful not to be confused;
Go forward step by step, be careful not to move backwards.

Go after them straight as Sher Shah,[161]
    Go in secret and in public.
Go with the power of *Allah*,
    Go after the enemy.

O sons of the brave! it can be done today but not tomorrow;
Go forward step by step, be careful not to move backwards.

For the sake of holy Islam,
    with pure intentions,
For the sake of religion,
    you have done all this for your nation as well.

O sons of the brave! Don't be negligent;
Go forward step by step, be careful not to move backwards.

Don't leave yourself open to taunts,
    either for your parents or grandfather.
For your relatives and strangers,
    defame the Khalqis and Parchamis yourself.

O sons of the high mountains! Don't argue amongst yourselves;
Go forward step by step, be careful not to move backwards.

I, Qatin, am praying for you
    at night and during the day.
I ask for your success;
    this is what I have to say to you.

O sons of our tribes! Don't sell yourselves to the Americans;
Go forward step by step, be careful not to move backwards.

Qatin
September 1, 2008

Give me your Turban

Give me your turban and take my veil,
Give me the sword so that the matter will be dealt with.

You stay at home; I am going to the battlefield,
I will either free my dear land, or we will make a new Karbala.

Don't just call yourselves men, how long will you lie there
    asleep?
You sit among the girls; may calamity fall down on your
    masculinity.

Leave these long tales and don't get so emotional,
Your cunning, truths and lies make me laugh.

The land which was set on fire is ablaze;
What would you know about widows and orphans?

That day will be my *Eid* and happiness,
When the enemy of my religion and land walks into the trap of
my influence.

To he who will build my ruined land, and establish a rule of what
is true,
Will such a person come to life? Will such a person appear?

I, Nasrat, am living in sorrow, the joyless life,
I will know the joy of life once my prayer is accepted.

Ms. Asefi Nasrat
September 15, 2008

Love of God

Don't talk of leaving the fortresses with me;
I don't care for death, don't talk about the knife.
I've come out to sacrifice myself to God;
I am pleased to burn, don't talk about fire.
I am the sign of morning, I attack the heart of darkness;
I go up in brightness, don't talk of dark nights.
Until the very end, I wage *jihad* with the enemy;
Don't talk of compromise and schemes to me.
I determine my own fate by fighting in fortresses;
Don't talk of the decisions of my rivals to me.
It doesn't matter if it is cut, let it be;
Don't talk of bowing down to others to me.
I will raise the flag of Islam with my blood;
I devote myself, don't talk of injuries.
I've come out against colonialism with my sword;
Don't talk of returning until I succeed.
As long as an Islamic government is not installed,
Don't talk to me about laying down arms.
Spring will come, the buds of freedom will smile,

Autumn will pass, don't talk of the falling of the leaves.
Today or tomorrow, Zahid says, the morning will come,
So don't talk of the gloom and the darkness.

Zahid

Ghazal

At a time when the tongue of songs grows mute and the
    musician becomes sleepy,
At a time when the Imam brings his faith,

At a time when the musician lights up the night with the rubab
    and sleeps in ignorance,
At a time when the breeze joins in the call for prayer,

At a time when the sparrows sit in line on the mosque's tree,
At a time when the child arrives with the *Qur'an* in order to
    learn it,

Some will keep their faith in the darkness of this test.
Some lose their faith and bring loss instead.

One will join the creator; he will be martyred in public;
The good news of a lover's fulfilment will come simultaneously
    along with separation

I am picking the rose, but the thorn will hurt my hand;
The competitor's turn comes at the same time as the beloved.

I will consider him a competitor and try to grab a hold from the
    neck;
I will reach his heart as well once I have his neck in my hand.

Sometimes I have a hard time distinguishing friend from foe;
The pagan arrives for war along with the Muslim.

At this point, a new fight will begin at honourable Maiwand;
Malalai will arrive together with Ayyub Khan.

O maiden of our homeland! Your happiness and grief on the
    same day!
Tears flow down past the lip and *pizwan*.

Looking forward to seeing the anxious and tired beloved.

Abdul Hai Mutma'in

O Afghan!

O Afghan, stand up! The enemy has come today;
He has come to the green lawn of your homeland.
Stand against him, you might destroy him;
He has come to the garden of red flowers.
Grab your sword and go to the battlefield;
Each of your enemies has come to your homeland.
Be careful not to turn your back;
A great arrogance has come to your homeland.
O Kamran, run like a lion!
A great tiger is sitting on your turf.

Mohammad Nabi Kamran

O Eid of the Trench

You came in peace, O *Eid*,
Joyful and blissful *Eid*.
I welcome your coming;
Come all the time, O *Eid* of Tor Ghar.[162]
We spent the month of fasting in the trench;
We walked in hunger.
Today, now that you are our guest, my dear
We will certainly celebrate you, *Eid* of Spin Ghar.[163]
But don't get upset, dear *Eid*;
Evening is near, O *Eid*.
We are moving to an ambush now,
The Western army is on the way, O *Eid*.
If we didn't honour you,
Don't get upset, O *Eid*.
O *Eid*, now are the days of revolution.
There is danger in every direction.

Don't complain to the *mujahedeen*.
They have many difficulties, O *Eid*.
Faizani is on the way
RPG on his shoulder, O *Eid*.

Rezwanullah Faizani
October 4, 2008

The Message of a Devoted Mujahed

The reason we always fold our moustaches upwards[164]
Is because we break the necks of our enemies.

We are all united. Our path and our movement is united.
We fold our white turbans and black *pahj* on our heads.[165]

We are happy when we are martyred for our extreme zeal and
 honour;
That is the reason we strap bombs around our waists.

We have properly identified the puppets and servants of the
 foreigners;
We circle their names in red on our lists.

The reason our bodies are porous from head to toe
Is because we strap chains to our arms and chests.

It is likely that we are drunk and no one can stare at us,
Because we will punch them flat on their mouths.

If we attack the checkpoints and bases of the enemies,
At midnight we encircle them with our soldiers.

We all are devotees for the sake of God, our beloved.
We do not care for death when we have our heads in our hands.

March 25, 2007

The Malalai of the Time

Which way did you go again?
For which peace did you go?

O Malalai, princess of the country,
To which mourning ceremony did you go, crying?

Your poems and love stories are not to be found there,
To which trench did you go to watch?

Your song of freedom is not to be found there;
For which Karbala of honour did you go again?

Roll up your sleeves,
Remember your beloved's memories.

Raise your voice for the honour of the homeland;
Become Malalai once more and raise the flag.

Teach *jirga*s to the *jirga* people;[166]
Become the voice of peace and memorise songs.

I want to hear your poems again;
I want to hear your cry of bravery.

O my love's poet!
O Husseinkhel's artist poet!

Husseinkhel
October 19, 2008

Suggestion

Move youth! Get ready for some committed work;
Make education your hobby and get ready with your pen.
Look at your culture; the foreigners are looting it;
Save history; destroy this dust.
Our heroes are being condemned by worthless people;
Destroy this decision of the foreigners with your work.
Look at this Cold War: from where is it imposed upon us?
Its propagators are sitting here; warn them with your pen.

The parliament is made up of foreigners, elected by us, though;
They have chosen the way of opposition amongst the people.
It is a pity for a party to be formed in opposition to the people:
It is made up of foreigners and it is built by foreigners.
Make yourselves aware of your history, O maidens and youths!
Ominous thoughts are at work, start your scientific struggles;
These impudent ones won't leave just with a few words.
They have hateful wishes; but surround them with your pen
O son of Ghazi Aman! O son of Wazir Akbar!
Take Mirwais' turban and inflict blows with Ahmad's sword.
Your pride is known in swords; take the pen O brave one!
Today is a world of education and science; beat the enemy in this
   way.
What would this Pedram know; he is directed by others;
If he is not Afghan then count him a puppet of others.
So if you want to beat them, make them look bad in knowledge;
Their roots will be erased; get ready for knowledge and a
   profession.
Accept Rafiqi's suggestion; this is the way, accept it.
Join with the books; end these troubles of yours.

Ustad Hayatullah Rafiqi
August 23, 2008

Strike the enemies of our village with stones!

Strike the enemies of our village with stones!
Youths! Be alert! They are spying on our village.
Depart for *jihad*; this is a legal obligation.
Kill the traitors of the village in the mountains.
The army of the crazed crusaders will withdraw
If our zealous *ghazis* fight.
We send messages of *jihad* to the West and to the East;
The loins of our village will come to the field in scores.
Mansour! The brave nation of Ayyub will succeed
If the faithful villagers support the *jihad*.

Mansour
December 16, 2007

Otherwise!

Otherwise?
Look! Don't call me brother.
Don't talk to me about village and home.
I will put up with handcuffs and shackles
And days and nights in prison.
You can enjoy sleeping on soft pillows and the *palang*[167],
You can go on *hajj* and fast, spend a long time praying,
But, will we enter and stay in paradise together?!

Bring out the weapons, O King!

You must be tired by now, take a break.
For God's sake stop it and repent.
If you really want peace for us.
Bring out the weapons, O King!
This is his fortieth night.
Take out some sweets for the martyred son.

Victory is very close for me.
O Malalai, come soon and recite a heroic poem.
It's enough my beloved; it's my fault.
But you should just take the hate from your heart.
No matter if you don't have gold or silver,
Give *zakat* from your straw.[168]

Basirullah Hamkar
August 3, 2008

My nation breaks the bloody heads

My nation breaks the bloody heads;
The enemy breaks the bangles of our girls;
They break their water pots while they are going to the spring.
I will take revenge with my blood for them;
They smash the foreheads of our people without guilt;
I swear that I'll bring earthquakes to your home.
My nations' sons always break down the foreigners;
Not only the youths but also my maidens break their heads;

150

Like Malalai who defeated the army of the British.
Anybody who glances the wrong way at my land will lose his
    head;
My nation breaks the bloody heads;
This is the home of honour, zeal and majesty.
We smash in the teeth of all our enemies;
O Nasrat, make sure to travel with the Pashtuns;
He who travels in the wake of the stranger will surely be bitten
    by dogs.

Nasrat
June 27, 2008

He walks

Love's enemy will walk in hiding from us;
We are the hunters; our prey walks in hiding from us.
He who would wander, riding on the throne of arrogance,
He is now scared and restless, walking secretly from us.
The many moments of relaxation that had been taken from us,
We will take them back; they are in a hurry, walking in hiding
    from us.
We have always prevented invaders,
We stand against them; they repeatedly walk in hiding from us.
Ah, weren't the stories of the English and Genghis in your
    mind?[169]
They walk in hiding as they escape from us.
Remember not to forget the Russians and Khalqis and
    Parchamis,[170]
They were embarrassed and helplessly walk in hiding.
We have become a Moses to all the Pharaohs of time:
We throw them to the Nile river; they walk in hiding.
Our friends made fun of us yesterday,
The infidels will do this a lot; they walk in hiding.
This invader enemy won't resist;
They are scared and walk in hiding.
No one will count our child among a group of children,
Their children will be few in number; they walk in hiding.
They were accusing us of being loveless;
They themselves are disgusted with love; they walk in hiding.
Those who didn't care about the country and sat in their houses,
They act like women and are walking in hiding from us.

Those whom we truly accompanied,
They are the real traitors and are walking in hiding from us.
Tahsin accepts all these games with the eyes of love;
He is right to be unhappy in his work, walking in hiding from us.

Tahsin
March 17, 2008

Flames

The Pharaoh of our time seems weak to me
From when I saw the youths in the trench.
My patience became heated
When I remembered the Abdalis through history.[171]
I see a light dawning with flames,
I saw the children of the *mujahedeen*.
Others aren't to blame; blame yourself!
I saw the enemies in the country.

Tahir Barakzai

Don't Come

Stop your complaints, stop your crying;
It is not out of enmity that I am not coming.
There are mines placed on the pathways and alleys;
The area around the mosque has been made "western".
Today in the morning, in that cemetery,
There were red, red wolves.
They didn't know Pashtu;
Their eyes were closed; they bit everybody.
Their mouths were shut; they were talking with their guns;
They told us not to come to this village anymore.
They said, there is nobody in this village today;
Jihad is in progress here.

Mirwais Jalalzai
September 23, 2008

Crusader Army

It's the crusader army, it can't tell *mihrab* from *minbar*;[172]
They have come out of the dark, they don't know light.
It is an open-mouthed dragon hungry for human flesh;
It is a flood of red blood and we can't tell mountain from level
    ground.
They are wild animals that came out of the forest;
They don't know any other art aside from war and fighting.
There are gunpowder flames and smoke from the bombs;
Bullets are falling everywhere and you can't tell east from west.
Flame falls on them, falls on them, O the thunder of the sky!
The devoted *mujahed* doesn't know death.
The lamp lights the blood on the path to independence;
A believer doesn't know any other cup except that of martyrdom.
We will go to the beach on the boat of *jihad*.
You are Muslim and don't know any other army except the
    *ghazi*s;
May you, Barialai, always be the hero of high steeds.
A *mujahed* never knows another leader.

Barialai Mujahed
July 17, 2008

Daughter of the West

A calamity has emerged from the Western gloom;
Blood is streaming in every direction; America has come out.
Heads are lying in every place, body parts are coloured red with
    blood;
The gunpowder strip is red; Europe has come out.
A group of animals called NATO have come out;
The Crusader world has come out for the murder of Jesus.
They have ruined human villages; they are throwing bombs at
    them;
There are taking out the roots of Islam; cholera has come.
They are sitting at Pharaoh's throne with arrogance;
Woe is here from the house of the oppressed nation.
An showcase of blood is presented along with the music of
    groans;
The red daughter of the West has come out; she dances naked.
They seek logic from the barrels of guns;

This speech has come from the Western culture's text.
Talk with the language of flames; put steps on the fiery footprint;
O *mujahed*, endlessness has come from this platform.

Barialai Mujahed
August 3, 2008

Ghazal

Sometimes they are shot by our people and sometimes by
    foreigners;
They are shooting Kabul cruelly.
He puts one hand over his eyes,
And with the other hand he fires and shoots a disabled man.
Look at this trick of the black calamity;
They shoot Afghans themselves.
Anybody who fires on our homeland
In fact is shooting at the heirs of our Malalai.
This black snake is full of poison;
He doesn't leave Afghans alone, shooting them many times.
Time will bring a Moses to stand next to the Pharaoh,
He who shoots at a great country.
Some are blind and can't see this;
Burn those who always shoot at our homeland.

Shamshir Hewad

The cries of forty-one countries reach the sky

The cries of forty-one countries reach the sky[173]
As their coffins leave our land to every location.

I wonder what might be written as a memory on their tombs?
Which nation led them to this end!

This is the result of their policy and of democracy;
Their work in Kabul and Baghdad has made them tremble.

They played with humanity's integrity to such an extent that
The brutality and barbarism of history must start crying.

The blow of Afghan shoes in an Afghan style!!
Muntazir Zaidi's message reaches every Afghan.[174]

God, these are all considered your mercy and examination;
An epic with an empty hand reaches a grand work.

We haven't stepped in anyone's house;
Inside the house, my message reaches the great slave.

Stop this puppetry and lowly life;
Your current position cannot achieve a firm hold.

As you present a medal to the dog with a name;
Your insult in the shape of a dog approaches *ghazi* Amanullah.

Be prepared for Afghan accountability and that of *Allah*;
Your name will surely reach as far as the trash can.

Aadil
January 5, 2009

Maiwand

Whether in the city or the mountains, it's our village;
There are screams and forces in our village once more.
They are ready to revolt once more;
Our entire village has become a trench – a trench – once more.
Somebody must have prayed for them;
Our village has become Maiwand and Khyber once more.
The small stones of our village once more;
Our village has great tribes – tribes – once more.
I know they have strong intentions;
Whether our village is in the east or the west.
Don't say spring won't come again;
Our village has this firm belief.
Stanizi isn't just making this up;
In fact, our village is actually this brave.

Stanizi
May 23, 2008

Poem

Who am I? What am I doing?
How did I get here?
There is no house or love for me;
I am homeless, without a homeland.
I don't have a place in this world;
They don't let me rest.
There are shots fired, and gunpowder here,
A shower of bullets.
Where should I go, then?
There is no place for me in this world.
A small house
I had from father and grandfather,
In which I knew happiness,
My beloved and I would live there.
They were great beauteous times;
We would sacrifice ourselves for each other.
But suddenly a guest came;
I let him be for two days.
But after these two days passed,
The guest became the host.
He told me, "You came today.
Be careful not to return tomorrow."

Najibullah Akrami
November 28, 2008

Trenches

Hot, hot trenches are full of joy;
Attacks on the enemy are full of joy.
Guns in our hands and magazine belts over my shoulders;
Grenades on my chest are full of joy.
The enemy can't resist when he sees them;
Black hair and stiff moustaches are full of joy.
He who fights in the field is manly;
Houses full of black-haired women are full of joy.
We become eager two times after hearing it:
The clang, clang and rockets are full of joy.
Leave the lips and spring, O poet!
Poems full of feeling are full of joy.

Jawad, I say, on the true path of *jihad*,
All kinds of troubles are full of joy.

Jawad
May 21, 2008

Poem

It is good to compete on every battlefield;
It is good that our brave blood is sprinkled out.
For those on whom the competitors count,
It is good that brave arms are strong.
When heart talks to heart,
It is good that lips are silent at that time.
As we relieve the evening headache with hashish,
Then it is good that these taverns are closed.
Feda takes joy from what is bitter;
It would be good to put poison in their mouths.

Maiwand Feda
September 19, 2008

Night Raid

Those who have ruined my life's harvest
Made a night raid on my home again.
The Red armies came and returned defeated;
They left the destroyed Afghan valleys behind them.
In any direction that I look, I see the deserted gardens;
The unity of my home has been hit by separation.
Who made a night raid on my home again?

* *

What complaint can you make of the Red, this is their rule;
The forest wolves will always eat meat.
What else should humans expect from the wolves?
They have hit my mount and Hamun's as well.
Who made a night raid on my home again?

* *

Somebody extended the hand of the cruel onto my lap,
That's why there is no respect for the country's *Ulemaa'*.
The turbans fell from the heads of our elders today,
They have set our people on fire.
Who made a night raid on my home again?

* *

The house of my history and culture was looted today,
Each slave is now riding me.
The teeth of the East and West have become like pliers on my
    muscles.
I have stepped into his hall in his presence.
Who made a night raid on my home again?

Wise up, O Afghan!
This scene of grief is made for you.
Be zealous and grab him by his neck,
This is seared on your heart from the history of yesterday.
Who made a night raid on my home again?

                                                  August 8, 2008

The Waiting Bullet

The moon remains behind the clouds,
The tent is waiting.
Evening is close, someone will come;
The white sign of waiting hangs.
A youth wipes his sweat here,
A cart stands beside him.
There is no chewing gum in the bag;
Wheat is in it now, the bag is standing.
She performed the prayer in a dark room;
A bareheaded old woman is standing.
She has put her hands on the holy *Qur'an*;
With open hands she is standing.
She wants peace for her supplication;
High on the roof she is standing and praying.
Tiredness passed, the youth became cheerful;
In front of him, a smiling blossom is standing.
A grey dog is standing nearby;

A hungry goat is looking at its feet.
Behind him, a yellow boy is standing;
Dawn is close, a knock on the door.
The youth went out, the group is standing;
It's the gun of the others, the uniform of the others.
A small group of those people are standing;
They take him; the house grows full of noise and shouting.
A bullet stands in every barrel,
Tears are falling on his collar.
The moon is standing at the depth of the water;
Years passed but in this heart
The entire world is waiting, it's not moving.

Nawa Jan Baheer
September 19, 2008

Feeling

I am in pain; I feel as I am alive.
O enemy! You burnt me with fire.
One day I will overcome you.
I am just sitting here, waiting for you.
(I feel like I am in hell.)
You tore my unspoiled country into pieces,
You made me feel ill, to have heart attacks.
You made my nation wander around destitute,
I will tear your collar into pieces.
Closed eyes don't watch over the war,
I will cut off your head and lay it at your feet.
I will run, making moves towards you,
I, Hemat, will hang you from the gibbet.

Hemat
December 16, 2007

Extreme Cruelty

O God! We experienced much suffering,
Many different tragedies we experienced.
When we tolerate one, the other attacks,
The *kuffar* come with their armies bearing down on us.

They have made every gentle human being cry;
As huge as any from the River Nile, we felt the waves.
Each one of us started to cry and weep,
A torrent of bullets we experienced.
Our country and houses were destroyed,
In a green garden we experienced the autumn.
O God! We hold up our hands and are praying to you;
In happiness we experienced grief.
Our body parts were scattered on the ground,
Huge aircraft flew over us.
What will calm the heart of Hamza,
When, more than anyone else, we have experienced pain?

Hamza
December 16, 2007

The White House

What a black ending the "White House" left behind:
Its whiteness turned black and it left behind a black evening.

Its black storm destroyed the well and broke the water pot;
This is the reason the girls left the house and village behind.

To their crown a necklace was also added;
Their condition was to become a servant, so I left my position.

O you who tread the path where the British, Genghis and the
    Russians have proceeded,
Here, with each step you pass a skull.

Their hangover vanishes when they see the angry forehead of the
    cup-bearer;
The hangovers in the tavern left full cups behind.

To those who watch gunpowder and blood and cries:
The doves of the heart of Haqyar left the roof behind.

Hassan Haqyar
January 5, 2007

160

Death is a Gift

I will never accept a life where I must bow to others;
I will never back the illegitimate for any money.

When the servants grant me something for spying;
I am repentant, I will never appeal to such national heroism.

Those who have one mouth but utter fifty different words and
    have fifty different thoughts
Like Karzai; I will not behave like a juggler.

I will not swear on Washington as my *qibla* nor will I bow to
    Bush;
Like some, the instructors who do this suffer.

I will not kiss the hand of Laura Bush, nor will I bow to Rice;[175]
I will not follow Gailani or Qanuni.[176]

My beliefs and my Pashtun pride teaches me this:
Even if I am chopped into pieces I will not beg from others.

If I can win the pearl of my hometown;
I would give up my life for the stone, I will not spare my head.

I sacrifice my head and my blood for the oppressed people;
But I will not even pretend to be humble in front of Pharaoh.

If I am mentioned like Shah Shuja, Babrak and Karzai in
    history,[177]
I will accept death but not a monarchy like this.

I will go and write on the gate to Panjshir;
I will not serve others as servants like you.

Tariq! What can the enemy do besides taking your life;
Death is a gift and I thank God for that.

Tariq Ahmadzai
January 5, 2007

Death's Slumber

I am not sure if everyone is blind;
They are all hit with death and in death's slumber.
They don't have eyes and their ears have become deaf;
Who knows whether they will get lost today or tomorrow.
The foreigners' army has surrounded the wall and doors;
They're being hit from all directions.
They don't open their eyes to see what's going on around them;
They don't see tomorrow and only live for today.
Their coffin is on their shoulders while they are alive;
This is death's slumber and deserves a burial.
The ones who are awake are drunk and high;
The sons of Abdal, Ghilzai and Zee themselves talk.[178]

Feda Mohammad Nawmir
August 23, 2008

Shrine of Martyrs

O pious God! Bring happiness and welfare to the sweet land of
    Afghans.
This temple of God's acceptors, this shrine of martyrs.
Beauty, His name is engraved on the heart of history;
This passage of invaders, this grave of occupiers.
How will the conquerors be able to climb the peaks of Your high
    mountains?
The flags of enemies have always fallen here.
Historically, idol-breakers have been fostered in Your cradle;
Birthplace of conquerors, training centre of the influential.
Each inch of Your land is smeared with red blood;
You! The country of heroes, You! The fortress of the faithful;
You honourably accepted the warm steps of the *ghazis*;
You insult the puppet servants by throwing soil on their faces
    and heads.
Metal and faith have clashed against each other here many times;
The atheists have gained nothing but defeat.
You altered storms; the entire world is indebted to You;
You, companion of the poor, You, leader of the hopeless.

December 4, 2007

Couplets

May I be sacrificed to the *mujahed*'s voice,
His *Allahu Akbar* shout shakes the infidels.[179]
I sacrifice myself to the dust of your feet,
Because the holy *Qur'an* swore on it.
I am proud of your martyrdom;
How happy I would be with a cowardly life.
My heart will be happy
When I see White House turn red with blood.
O mother of the martyred, you are lucky
Because they bury your martyred son with his clothes.
O God, for these tears of the martyred man's sister,
Turn them to a flood to destroy the infidels.
As I saw the martyrs' sisters,
They were thanking God.
I sacrifice myself to your dismembered corpse;
The angels of heaven have prepared medals for you.
Many angels came down from the sky
To collect the pieces of your holy corpse.

Mohammad Gadakhil

Speech to the *Mujahedeen*

Thanks be to God,
    we have many followers on the path of *jihad*.
We have many devotees
    to sacrifice themselves for the sake of religion.
We have many responsible youths
    ready to sacrifice themselves.
Each one is in a hurry, saying
    "We want to sacrifice ourselves first".
They are heading to
    the fortress of *jihad*.
We have plenty of flowers
    in the gardens of the country.
Their parents don't know of them;
    they are ready for *jihad*.
We have plenty of opportunists:
    obstinate, brave men.

163

They are reminded of marriage
   and taking part in happiness.
They say, "we prefer to be martyred."
   "we will have plenty of *houri*s and handsome boys."
They fly like falcons
   and fly over high mountains.
They take their positions over the peaks;
   we have plenty of hawks.
We have educated,
   well-experienced people.
They don't make pretexts;
   we have plenty of devotees.
In life they have
   Everything they could ever need.
We have such zealous men.
They hope for martyrdom,
   receiving wounds in their chest.
We have plenty of brave youths
   who are ashamed to receive wounds in their back.
They hope for martyrdom,
   that it is granted by God as a gift.
We have plenty of youths
   to accept such gifts.

Rafiq
December 16, 2007

Tomorrow is the day of *Eid*

Tomorrow is the day of *Eid*;
May *Allah* make it blissful.
Someone will be sitting next to someone else;
Someone will be taking care of the trench.
Someone will be going paired with the foreigners;
In which mountains will the zealous youths be living?
Some will be sitting with their families in happiness;
Some will be crying for their imprisoned son.
Some will be away making money in other places;
Some will be on the journey of *jihad*.
With death at every step,
Afghan youths will spread horror for them:

Some will chase the enemy on the way;
Amanzai has taken Lowgar for them.

Amanzai
October 1, 2008

Verse

Sometimes, we devote our life to the homeland,
Sometimes, we do something for the Afghan nation
Sleep comfortably and wake up;
Safeguard the birthright of your ancestors.
You are the offspring of Ghaznawi; think about it.
Break the statues of Sumanat again.[180]
Why did you forget the achievements of your ancestors?
Declare the history of Ahmad Shah.
Safeguard the garden of Mirwais Khan with your blood;
Defend the dignity of the veil of Malalai now.
There is autumn in our country; we die with the hope of spring;
Bring the spring to this country!
My friend! Safeguard the dignity of your homeland in the world;
Drive out the crow from this garden.
Day and night, you walk in other people's homeland;
Pay a visit to poor Afghanistan.
Be ready to discover the devilish actions of the enemies;
Do not demolish your homeland.
I presented you a few parts of devices;
Give my regards to Sarachawal.

Matiullah Sarachawal
December 4, 2007

Afghanistan is the home of Afghans

Afghanistan is the home of Afghans;
It is the home of the brave and courageous.
Foreigners won't be able to weaken it by force;
This is the home of Mirwais' sons.
These people defeated Brydon's armies;[181]
This is the home of Macnaghten's murderers.
They gave an embarrassing defeat to the Russians;

Gromov admits that this is the home of victors.[182]
Tribes and clans are found here;
This is the home of the Hazaras and Turkmen.
Tajiks, Uzbeks, Pashtuns and Baluch;[183]
This the home of devoted Afghans as well.
These mountains are ours and we belong to these mounts;
This is the home of the eagles.
Jackals can't hold out here;
This is the home of *Allah*'s great lions.
Ahmad Shah's sword did not cool down yet;
This is the home of the followers of the right religion.
These are the sons of Ghouri and Ghaznawi;
This is the home of those heroes.
Great Jamaluddin Afghan;[184]
This is the home of his followers.
These people give their heads for their religion;
This is the home of Islam's servants.
The invading forces will eventually leave;
This is the home of strong heroes.

Dardmand
August 26, 2008

Lolling

Rabbits have confused themselves and are lolling with the
    camels;
Eagles left their nests and are hanging out with the ravens.
Look at these ewes and goats, how immodest they have become;
They prowl with the wolves in the light of day.
They slaughtered all their young children yesterday;
Today, those without zeal are consorting with the Khalqis.[185]
I said they would ruin this country all on their own
Because I saw the *mujahedeen* meeting with the Parchamis.
What happened to a zeal for power, O friends?
Sunnis are relaxing in groups with the Shi'a.[186]
This shame will damage your reputation too, O Khalis;
Instead of the Russians they are lolling with the Westerners now.

Mawlawi Yunis Khalis
July 25, 2008

Islam's Heroes

Whoever has received the blow of an Afghan sword to his head,
Never resisted or escaped from the battlefield.
His brave sword is clear to the entire world,
So much so that the red infidels ran from his homeland.
This is the soil of Islam; it has well-trained heroes;
This is why they would have beaten the enemy on any ground.
This homeland has reared and trained religion's heroes,
Each one placed in the crib of zeal by their mothers.
The entire Muslim world is proud of their *mujahedeen*
Because they have brought shame to the name of Communism
    around the world.
You erased Lenin's communist system from the world;
It was scattered in such a way that the whole universe laughs at
    them.
Look at history, which each Afghan has in the background:
The English are a great example of those who have been pushed
    out.
Afghans made sacrifices for their honour;
They made a revolution; each traitor is shaken by them.
Nations are amazed by Afghans,
Since they have beaten a power like Bush.
Afghan sons don't have any parallel, O Ahmad Yar!
Stop complimenting them, they are victorious in every field.

Hanif
October 28, 2008

Voice

We saw people as they were being buried;
We saw the prisons as they became full.
They put many youths into the black dust;
We saw them as they pulled out people's nails.
Suddenly the army of Ayyub appeared;
We saw the traitors as they were swelling.
Mujahed Malik shouted *Allahu Akbar*!
We saw the Russians as they fled.
The Ghazis' *Allahu Akbar* voice spread;
We saw the offices as they were established.

167

They took our swords and shields;
We saw the English as they were coming.
O Wayand, this simplicity is good;
We saw the bodies as they grew fat.

Wayand
May 21, 2008

Pamir

I know the black, black mountains;
I know the desert and its problems.
My home is the mountain, my village is the mountain and I live
    in the mountains;
I know the black ditches.
I always carry a rocket-launcher on my shoulder;
I know the hot trenches.
I always ambush the enemy;
I know war, conflict and disputes.
I will tell the truth even if I am hung on the gallows;
I know the gallows and hanging.
I don't care about being hot or cold;
I know all kinds of trouble.
I am the eagle of Spin Ghar's high peaks;
I know Pamir's canyons.
I walk through it day and night;
I know the bends of Tor Ghar.
Bangles are joyful on the girls' hands;
I know swords.
Those who make sacrifices for religion;
Faizani, I am familiar with such young men.

Faizani
May 21, 2008

Warriors

When the infidels appear, they tremble;
When they see the *ghazis*, the *ghazis*.
I am going to the trench, I will do *jihad*;

See Nuristan today, see Nuristan today.
When I remember the *ghazi*, I sacrifice myself to him;
I am always going to see the *ghazi*.
Now see Laghman, now see Laghman;
This is the praise of *ghazi*s, it's popular among Afghans.
Its mountains are graves and its pets are its young men;
Look at the people of Kunar now; look at the people of Kunar
now.
Mukhlis is happy in the trench seeing infidels scattered;
Look at the people of Nangarhar now; look at the people of
Nangarhar now

Zahid ul-Rahman Mukhlis

This Country Will Be Freed

This country will be freed because the *ghazis* are fighting in it;
Everywhere there will be freedom for individuals and the
takbirs[187] will be heard.
But near each door there will be a fortress and an army of *ghazis*
as well;
And the enemies would be found guilty for they have turned the
earth into the Day of Judgement.

Everyone's head will be broken and the *ghazi* sword will sweep
through the air;
All tribes will gather together and again they will occupy the
forts.
Each one's *shimla*[188] will be raised along with bushy beards and
white faces;
Everyone's eyes will get red and the enemies will be scared.

This country will be freed because the *ghazis* are fighting in it;
Everywhere there will be freedom for individuals and *takbirs* will
be heard.
But near each door there will be a fortress and an army of *ghazis*
as well;
And the enemies would be found guilty for they have turned the
earth into the Day of Judgement.

This will be a new revolution in which every cruel person will
 suffer;
Each criminal will be ashamed and taken to trial.
This flood will clear the dirt and will spread in every direction;
The oppressed will become happy and everywhere there will be
 freedom.

Everyone will break their chains and every captive's hand will be
 freed;
In order to gain independence for the nation; the countrymen
 will smile.

January 1, 2007

Home of Heroes

My lord, build the homeland of the poor Afghans,
This residence of the zealous and brave believers.
Your light has been written in the golden pages of history,
How the enemies would capture the peaks of your mounts!
The disgraced flag of the infidels has always fallen here;
The heroes of history have grown up in your bosom.
You are the homeland of the Afghans and the graveyard of the
 enemies;
Every part of your soil is stained with the blood of the martyrs.
You are the homeland of the victors; you are the home of the
 heroes;
Infidel and Muslim have been crushed here many times.
The unbelievers have always been defeated on your soil;
When storms came towards you, you stood out in front of them.
The entire West is in your debt for the defeat of the Russians;
When it's time for their fall, then they come towards you.
Now, the caravan of the crusaders has come to your bosom,
Abedzai says that the cross will break in your bosom.
The white flag of faithful Afghans will be hoisted once again.

Mawlawi Samiullah Abedzai
September 1, 2008

Good News

These are days of insolence and the White House's collapse;
These are days of the collapse of the infidels' coalition.
The signs of disunity appear among these forces;
These are days of the unity of Islamic countries.
Bad Abraha has come to ruin our *ka'aba*;[189]
These are the days when the green birds come.[190]
For the Abrahamic nation that today they burn with fire,
These are the days when Nimrod's forces are burnt.
The Pharaoh of the time has come, is killing our children;
These are the days when the Satanic armies are drowned.
Bush arrived impudently and wouldn't listen to anyone;
His economy is ruined; these are days of happiness.
He didn't learn from Gorbachev's defeat;
He is disgraced in the world; these are days of shame.
For those who would go to their houses in the darkness of night,
These are the days when the wild forces escape.
They intentionally bombard and then make their excuses;
These are the days when the crusader terrorists disappear.
The Muftis of the invaders with white turbans,
They are embarrassed; these are days of crying.
Towards freedom with the help of *Allah*,
We are taking firm steps; these are days of hope.
Martyrs of the sweet homeland, tell us in our dreams:
Take revenge; these are days of uprising.
The world will remain; don't sell your faith in it, brothers;
The *houris* are waiting for you; these days are coming.
Abedzai requests martyrdom from *Allah*;
Life in this world is enough; these are days of disaster.

Mawlawi Samiullah Abedzai
December 19, 2008

White House

May you burn in red flames, White House;
May you burst into flames, turn to ashes, White House!

There are black calamities in your belly, you seem so white;
May you turn to ruins, White House!

The murderers of the oppressed tribes live inside;
May you turn red with their blood, White House!

You have been the centre of cruelty and barbarism since long
    ago;
May you collapse at your foundations, now, White House!

You took the faith away from those who love the West;
May you become the target of those who love Islam, White
    House!

May *Allah* fell you as it did Bush;
May you be plagued with Obama's grief, White House!

Ahmadi
January 29, 2009

Mujahed

You are a strange lion of the world, O *mujahed*!
You are the champion of the true path, O *mujahed*!
You attack like a lion in the trenches;
You are in fact the man of the field, O *mujahed*!
You beheaded many infidels;
The whole world knows you, O *mujahed*!
You played football with the heads of *infidels*;
You are in fact the son of an Afghan, O *mujahed*!
You sounded out the Islamic *kalima* to the world;[191]
You are a strange light of the time, O *mujahed*!
You have taken the path of Mohammad;
You sacrifice to the *Qur'an*, O *mujahed*!
Zahid makes himself busy complimenting you;
You are well-known in the histories, O *mujahed*!

Khalid Zahid

Fault

I am brutally murdered but no one tells me my fault;
I hope no one is shown the oppressed tears and effects by God.

Why have you placed the picture of the enemy in front of me?
My sweetheart! No one shows pork to a believer.

Yet, the time has not started when, to tell the truth;
The bright mirror does not reflect the picture in darkness.

The mouths of a few captives are closed and then killed one by
     one;
They prefer to accept death rather than to reveal their leader.

We know the past and the future will also pass;
It does not matter if the angels don't reveal our fate.

People keep secrets in their hearts and they don't reveal them;
Like you, oh prosperity! Do not show your inner self.

                                                    January 16, 2007

The Passing of the Crusaders

I'll go to my sweet homeland
When peace comes to my beloved homeland.
We won't travel in any other direction
Once the *shari'a* is ensured there.
I go there from time to time,
When it is time to farm our lands.
When I go there, my friends tell stories to me:
I was waiting for the bus, when I saw something;
Foreigners were in the back, the traitors ahead of them.
The crusaders passed with arrogance,
Like the wicked who pass by the poor.
The poor all stood aside
As if an eagle would come upon the birds.
The man with a little zeal would look with anger to them.
He can't do anything to them; sweat breaks out on his forehead.
They can't survive the *mujahed*'s remote gaze.
Once they see them through the binoculars,

173

How will these blue eyes survive in good health
When he is ambushed?
Oh Janbaz! Take revenge for the men of the country from them.
He is waiting for when the traitors come.

Janbaz
October 28, 2008

I wish

I wish my hands were able to reach the enemy,
And that my territory was protected...
I wish I wasn't needy and not like the living dead;
I wish we could take our injured fighters to physicians.
Come out like men to the battlefield and show yourselves;
I wish this scream could reach the president!
I wish I could take care of orphans and was rich;
I wish I was able to be kind to the orphans.
I wish I could tell Mohammad Stanikzai about myself;
I wish my voice reached the wind though my mouth is closed.

Mohammad Stanikzai
December 16, 2007

Hunter

O hunter! why did you hold the arrow in your bow?
You opened your closed eye slowly.
It looks like you started watching my youth.
Yes, I am that deer in this forest
To whom *Allah* has granted much beauty.
Why, hunter? You put the arrow back in the bow
And you put the bow back on your neck.
Yes, in this forest I am that deer,
Whose old friends are the minds of each star.
And each moment of mine is shared with the moon.
From time to time, on the fifteenth, the moon comes to me,
And sits on that side of the forest next to me.
Do you believe that it tells me all the stories
About what troubles have come to our homeland?

They are taking the maidens from you and you are looking at
    them;
What other misfortune are you still waiting for?
Your brides are leaving in coffins.
Why, hunter? You bend your head down
As if you were a vulnerable creature of this forest.
I trusted you, your bravery.
You have come after my prey to the forest.
Your sisters and mothers were taken by them.
They burned your *Qur'an*.
They destroyed the mosque in your village.
They cut the tongue that sang the *Azan* from the Mullah.
They unclothed all the elders of your village.
If you were a man, you with the arrow
In your bow, with one of your eyes closed,
You would kill an infidel with it.
But, O hunter! Now that you have come to this forest,
The lion is still the king and the jackal is still the slave.
If a dog comes to this forest from somewhere,
We count him as a dog and treat him as a dog.
A monkey is worthless and incompetent here,
This forest is much better than the homeland.
Your homeland is being controlled by the pigs.
They have brought a sick dog with them
To rule over your honour.
You have got rid of those lions,
Who beat the wolves of the Caucasus.
But hunter, take this from me:
Last night the moon told me
That you brought the nests of
A few eagles to your homeland.
You look for them each morning
You should remove the eyes of this dog.
There would then be such a young ruler
Whom the lions would fear.
You will hear the *Azan* again;
Worship will only be for the one God.
These jackals will be
Either killed or will flee.
So, hunter, go!
If you were a follower of the dog
Or a slave of the pigs
Then go and bow down.

175

Cry to God and repent
Because you won't
Arrive in your house from here yet.
Conditions will change
You will see on every path,
In every cave and ditch,
Those murdered pigs.
And those lions of the mountains
Will be walking in the cities.

September 8, 2008

Warning

I am a rough Afghan, I will not be deceived;
I cannot leave the circle of dignity.
If you slaughter more and more
I will not show up and become your servant.
If you chop me into pieces,
I will not lose my dignity in front of you.
It is part of my inheritance that
I cannot escape from the trench.
My blood has been stirred up;
I cannot accept coarseness.
I am a Muslim who has been granted Afghan zeal;
I cannot accept to become your agent.
The cruelties of Bush and Gordon Brown;
I cannot tolerate this for Afghans.
Turab is speaking to all the *kuffar*;
I cannot allow you to remain in my country.

Turab
December 16, 2007

The Human Cost

I live in flames

I live in thorns like a flower;
Like the butterfly, I live in flames.
If anyone asks you about me,
I am an Afghan living in the valleys.
I don't like anybody else's palaces;
I am the son of Afghans; I live in a tent.
When I see the country's wounds,
I start screaming and sigh.
I will always care about my country;
What happened to Afghans? I live in thought.
The enemy came and became our boss today,
My country was destroyed; I live in ruins.
My country cries aloud here,
That's why I live in grief once again.
Is there anyone who will wash away my tears?
I am Kabul, living in red flames.
Light has left my homeland,
I am falling in every direction; I live in the dark.
I am Watanyar, in mourning for my country,
I am awake each night until dawn.

Abdul Basir Watanyar
June 20, 2008

Homeland

My dear homeland is burning but I am watching.
Its soil and deserts are destroyed, I am watching.
This is cruel, O my creator! Build the homeland!
Afghans are leaving, I am watching.
I don't know who has plotted against our freedom.
My Afghan brother is crying, I am watching.
Shin Gul has cried with lukewarm tears.
Blood streams from the heart, I am watching.

Shin Gul Aajiz

Tears

As long as this situation continues,
Some will be poor and some will be wealthy.
Afghanistan will always be ruined.
Everybody cares only about himself.
This cruel dragon will remain here.
This oppressed nation will be ruined.
Our life will be tough.
This nation is in trouble.
Wardak's tears will continue to stream;
The enemies will be safe.

Wardak
June 27, 2008

I was Afghan; that's why I wasn't the hero

No matter that I didn't become a fellow traveller with anyone
    else,
But thank goodness that I haven't changed like the seasons.
Despite such a great victory, O people of the world,
I was Afghan; that's why I wasn't the hero.
What calamity has befallen my poor destiny?
I became a stranger to my relatives but didn't become the
    relative of strangers.
I looked unfaithful to myself back then;
I didn't become crazy in the separation.

Sa'adullah
August 8, 2008

Ababeel

Autumn came to you instead of spring, my homeland,
A hot wind and torrents of fire came down upon you.
Your blossoms of wishes have faded in this world,
Storms of cruelty and power came at you from all sides.
You were tired and exhausted from poverty,
The red wide-mouthed predator came at you.
You have seen the cruelties of the locals and the foreigners,

Wars, tension, murders and killings came upon you.
This world has become a hell for you; you are burning in it,
You haven't died so far, yet more bullets seek you out.
You have made many of your sons messengers to paradise,
Satan, the ambusher, came at you from afar.
They roasted you on the fire like a kebab once again,
Satan's puppet came at you bearing an Afghan name.
They brought the army again, they are not yet sated,
The great convoy – the Nimrod of its time – came for you.
Abraha's army with the arrogance of the West,
A row of their tanks and elephants came at you.
Your true sons will not give you a man-made paradise of this
    world,
Leader or *mujahed*, a sympathetic Afghan came upon you.

Rafiq
October 25, 2008

O *Eid*!

Swear to bring happiness when you come
Bring a portion of their peace to this poor nation.
But how would you come here
To become a cure for injured hearts?
There is grief here,
Here is mourning.
Here is crying and sorrow,
There is tumult in every home.
And you are *Eid*,
You are very prosperous.
You are the symbol of happiness,
The symbol of wealth.
You have the colour of henna about you,
Here we have colour, though not that of henna.
Here we have the red of blood and wounds;
That colour is on the hands of the widows and women whose
    sons are killed.
The sound that you hear is not the clinking of women's
    jewellery,
It is not the sound of happiness.
It is the sound of weapons and armour.

You are unaware; here is war, here is war.
About which desert should I cry to you?
Cry to you either about Laili or Bakwa?
Everywhere here is Karbala,
Everyday for us Ashura.
It is your choice: either you want to see your graveyard,
Or you want to see a prison built around knowledge.
You want to see Afghanistan
You want to see the *Amir* or the commander.
Their hands are tainted with blood, blood.
As you see every Afghan,
You see an Afghan son; You see a Muslim.

So, O *Eid*!
The source of happiness.
The thing that shows brotherhood,
You are the symbol of unity.
You are the tradition of the great Prophet;
If you are listening, don't come here.
We aren't ready for your arrival,
We don't have the patience of happiness.
No matter how great your impact is,
Our orphans are used to crying.
Let us cry,
Leave us to our sorrow.
Leave us for destruction,
Leave us to our destiny.
It's your choice then, whether you come or not,
Whether you accept the words of poor Mohsin or not.

So, O *Eid*,
Most fortunate;
O, unaware of our bad condition,
As you are coming, don't come with empty hands.
Don't come without emotion as in the past,
As you are coming, bring brotherhood.
Bring national unity,
Bring good health,
Bring good politics,
Bring love,
Bring abundance,
And.......and........and

Swear that you'll bring happiness when you come,
Bring a portion of peace to this poor nation.

Ahmad Hussein Enayat Mohsin
October 1, 2008

Quatrains

Let's hug each other;
Let's unite ourselves.
It is the time of love and brotherhood;
The time of hate has passed.

* *

My competitor cut my heart;
Tears streamed from my eyes.
O relentless one, your heart is harder than stone;
I weep for you and you laugh at me.

* *

It is the time for flowers and bushes;
A line of birds came from the upper side.
Life is about songs now;
We'll hit our rival with stones.

* *

We love these dusty and muddy houses;
We love the dusty deserts of this country.
But the enemy has stolen their light;
We love these wounded black mountains.

* *

The light that began shining from Hera
Spread all the way to Europe and Africa.
Mohammad brought a message of peace;
Barbarism, cruelty and oppression started to fade.

* *

The sun's rays cry out for my grief;
My heart's flower-like branches are broken.
Funerals are held for my wishes;
The rival looted what I invested in hope.

Nasrat

Afghans bring me to tears

The cruelties of the entire world bring me to tears;
Aside from my rival and the bearer of news, my beloved also
    makes me cry.
He rolls around in the soil with his bare head and feet,
These orphans of our country bring me to tears.
Autumn has made the flowers of the garden fall and wilt,
The nightingale's cries in the garden bring me to tears.
Pretty like parrots dispersed and wandering around,
Afghans wandering in other countries bring me to tears.
The *kuffar* don't permit me to be happy in my own country,
Ready with swords in hand, the cruel ones bring me to tears.
When I recall Malalai being injured, I feel regret,
But for now, they don't permit me; my own wishes bring me to
    tears.
I imagine any other country is beautiful like a flower,
Kabul smells of gunpowder, it brings me to tears.

Hayatullah Khaksar
December 4, 2007

Golden Pages

In this city, people escape from each other;
In this city, no one's wishes are fulfilled.
As long as your blood-thirsty eyes are still moving in their
    sockets
In this city, the killing will continue.
They will grow and grow green and spread the breeze;
In this city, I planted the seeds of an immature love.
The Khans, Nawaabs and leaders and rulers[192]
Each have given me injuries to my heart in this city.
I try to forget, but it is not possible; what should I do?

In this city, the golden pages of my life have been blown away by
 the wind;
God knows better where the wise and clever people have gone.
In this city, a few mad people walk around exhausted.
Previously, they were used for tying up branches and bouquets
In this city, now ropes are used for the gibbet.
O Majnun! Better to escape from this city now
Because humans are being cut into pieces.

Letter in Chains

You are brutalising them in chains, O cruel one,
That's why the poor are sighing in their chains.
You built the hateful prison in Cuba,
Giving electric shocks to the detainees in chains there.
If you brutalise them today in chains, the turn for us, the poor,
 will come too;
You will remember this in chains later on.
I am not complaining about others, my competitor sold me to
 them,
That's why I wish them all the worst in the chains.
You think we will give up when we are in chains, O my enemy!?
Muslims have learnt many lessons while they were in chains.
I follow my father's and grandfather's steps, I am going forward;
They spent several years in chains.
There were chains on their legs and chains on their hands,
Taking steps like children in the chains.
May you break these chains of brutality into pieces, O my
 Creator;
Your imprisoned lover is praying for you in chains.
If God wills it, these chains will break very soon;
I have seen my beloved imprisoned in chains.
O Angels of Paradise, allow rest and comfort for the lover in
 chains;
These martyrs have suffered a lot in chains.
You mentioned the troubles of the chains;
Maftoun has written that there are joys to be found in the chains.

Maftoun
September 1, 2008

Self-made Prison

Tears run down my collar, O God!
Afghan history has been defamed.
Just as our turban was held high in the world,
Today it has descended, O God.
The nightingales cry and remember their lawn,[193]
The foreigners brought autumn to it.
They are buying its honour and esteem with dollars,
All the competitors have unified against it, my God.
This madman is targeting them with stones,
They turned my wishes to dust.
It's a pity that we are wandering as vagrants,
We did all of this to ourselves.
A torrent of tears passes down my face
When I remember Afghanistan, my God.
Poor Afghans are suffering everywhere,
There is no one to ask about them, my God.
Where would we go, to whom would we cry, my God?
Say, ruin the cruel, my God.

Nasery
October 25, 2008

Prison Sighs

My brave brother!
My traveller friend!
My companion in *tawhid*![194]
Hey! My companion of the fortress!
Did you ever think of me?
Did you ever remember me?
My sympathetic brother for the sake of God!
Say! When food is laid out on the tablecloth for you
Do you remember my dry throat and lips?
When you go to your soft and pleasant bed
Do you imagine my handcuffs and shackles?
My traveller friend!
My companion in *tawhid*!
Say! Swear by the unity of the one God
When you arrive home
Your children gather together around you

185

Your wife sits down in front of you
Do you regret
The tears of my wife
And the screams of my children?
My old grandmother's sighs and tears?
Do you sometimes feel sorry for that?
Do they sometimes make you suffer?

Barialai Mujahed
December 4, 2007

Pul-i Charkhi Prison

May *Allah* come down upon your walls, O Pul-i Charkhi
    prison;[195]
Fear has seeped out of your courtyard once again.
May your stones and foundations be cast into the fires of hell;
You put foreigners' weapons on your shoulders to kill me.
Once again, cruel leaders turned their daggers red with our
    blood;
Once again, the disgraced have brought the tanks of the Western
    Satan.
The cloaked magician wanders like a beggar,
Trying to find some more forces to kill me.
The green parrots of the United Nations are mute;
Those who talk of Human Rights have sealed their mouths shut.
We are hooked up to our enthusiasm; look at our firm
    determination.
We don't fear death, nor suffer pain from our wounds.
We dedicate our heads to Islam.
May death come a hundred or a thousand times on this path.
Ahmadi says, O *Allah*, take our revenge from them!
Or make us stronger than them, to cut off their heads.

Qari Yousuf Ahmadi
December 19, 2008

Ghazal

The English are wandering on my soil,
Those red, red-faced infidels are wandering.
But it's a pity when I see
My Afghans wandering with them.
Cry for these widows and orphans,
Cry for my injured in the hospitals.
The legs of some and the hands of others are amputated;
Cry for my martyrs in the cemeteries.
I won't ever forget them;
A love of the *Qur'an* walks in my heart.
Those who were brokering the selling of countries,
The slaves of the English are wandering.
They play with my head today,
They are wandering with *pizwan.*
He taunts me today,
They are ashamed, wandering in the world.

August 3, 2008

They Put

Some set us on fire,
Some put us on spears.
Everybody showed us green gardens,
Then they put us on thorns.
We have been robbed by our relatives;
Now they blame the foreigners for it.
Many bronze lions are heroes now;
They put soil over the brave.
I am surprised by some of these people;
They still put guns on their shoulders.
O God! Save us from the cruel;
They poured soil over our hopes.

Safi
August 3, 2008

Childlike Shout

A childlike shout goes out of this city;
Tension and pain leave its bosom and wounds.
They brought their proud heads to the ground because of my
    dignity;
That man of contrivance leaves Kandahar.
The one who grows thorny sleep on my eyes;
The arrows of sighs leave my heart like stings.
My Afghan beauty is destroyed by the bad appearance of these
    green eyes;
My body's blood leaves me in a thorny stream.
Its fresh blossoms, green leaves weren't open yet;
The fresh branch now leaves the dust of compulsion.
Whatever you put in front of him,
Tears leave Basharat's eyes involuntarily.

Basharat
August 3, 2008

Couplets

We have put up with many difficulties,
We have wept in dark nights.
When we let out our screams,
One bitter word can hurt a hundred people.

* *

We were enflamed together with dry logs,
Wet wood never takes light.
I hope for our rescue from the fires of hell;
The pig put more fire on me here.

* *

I acknowledge we may not be gentlemen,
But, we didn't run away from the foreigners.
What does the foreigner think of us?
No one has driven us out of our own land.

December 16, 2007

Stones

When I cover my legs, my head is uncovered;
I was forced to remove my veil.
Your hands will be slit and covered in blisters.
Come! Put your fingers on my chest.
I was prevented from watching the nightingales
When my wing was broken in the sky.
I had dreamed of a large palang
But the desert's thorns became my bed.
It seems a sign of collapse to me;
O people! I am astonished.
I am astonished by the actions of Malik;[196]
When the stones are thrown, they hit my head.

Mir Ahmad
December 23, 2007

Three Interesting Quatrains

My competitor hits me with stones;
Tears line up one after another.

I am wounded at every moment;
Arrows fall upon the pages of my heart.

* *

My heart's rose got hurt, hurt.
The mosque was martyred and the *mihrab* was destroyed.

Each of my *ghazals* are filled with crying;
My life's book is red with blood.

* *

I don't know for what reason he is killing me;
These red and black ones are killing me.

I am sadder than if I had died myself that
The enemy is not killing me, they are killing my brother.

June 27, 2008

The Time of the Dollars

I am astonished at this time of the dollars;
In poverty, I lost friendship.
Elsewhere Muslims are drenched in blood;
The world became a jail for Muslims.
Alas! What people inherited me?
What a life, it's a hollow joke.
The poor are insulted by riches;
To be poor is a reason for disrespect.
Mukhlis says, for the sake of this sweet country,
My blood takes a vow to love.

Zahid ul-Rahman Mukhlis
December 23, 2007

Moan

What injured moaning is this that reaches my ear?
What sigh of the defenceless is shaking God's domain?
Which sister's veil is this that has fallen from her head?
And whose cruelty has made her hair dusty?
What punishment for crimes is this that you have fallen to pieces,
The implementation of whose law has thrown you to the dust?
Which bride's hand is this that is red with red blood?
Which sigh of the defenceless is shaking God's domain?
Which poor man's house is this that has been ruined by bombs?
Why has this cottage become the food of fire?
Which child's body is this that is smirched with red blood?
The smoke of whose wishes will rise again today?
Which stone's heart is this that is never satisfied?
Which sigh of the defenceless is shaking God's domain?
Which mother's scream is this that comes out of her mouth?

She is sitting by the dead body of her son, is standing and falling.
She has taken the bloody clothes to both her eyes.
Which heart's voice is this that directly enters into my heart?
Which brute's ears are these that are deaf to this?
Which sigh of the defenceless is shaking God's domain?
Because of which Pharaoh are his feet bare?
Children are shouting and are scared and terrorised today.
They don't eat or drink: they are alone.
They move to the dusty deserts out of fright from the brutal
    bombardment.
F.S. sees the houses of the poor being destroyed everywhere he
    looks.
Which sigh of the defenceless is shaking God's domain?

Dr. Faizullah Saqib

Injured

I stoned him with the stones of light tears
Then I hung my sorrow on the gallows like Mansour.
Like those who have been killed by the infidels,
I counted my heart as one of the martyrs.
It might have been the wine of your memory
That made my heart drunk five times.
The more I kept the secret of my love,
This simple *ghazal* spoke more of my secrets.
The one who gave you his trust,
That person neglected you.
I was injured, my brother was martyred,
My stepmother watched me.
O poem of Khairkhwa! I will accept your perfection
If you guide back one of those who have fallen astray.

Khairkhwa
June 22, 2008

Ghazal

What great times of happiness we had that have passed,
There was no sadness, no pain, but that time has passed.
When I go there I am reminded of those times,
There were ceremonies that passed.
How the saddened flower smiled once again,
There was an autumn breeze in the lawn which has passed.
There are no enjoyable speeches at gatherings,
The time had its joy, which has passed.
Don't be cheated by anyone's appearance in the future, my
    heart,
These were false colours that have passed.

Islam Ghani Orakzai

Immigration Problems

I feel sorry for you, my refugee brother,
O my refugee brother of flowers and troubles.
Feet with blisters, torn collar and injured hands,
May I be sacrificed for you, my zealous brother.
You accepted this enormous grief just for your honour and zeal,
O my great brave brother.
Your steps have taken you to many countries,
My upset and most deprived brother.
I find the mark of your hand on every brick of every building,
You are innocently lying in the desert, my thankful brother.
Your children expect comfort and blessings from you,
You sigh with empty hands, my pictured brother.
Many storms came down upon you,
My strong-willed and well-known brother.
I don't see you lacking any cruelty,
You are used to difficulties, my patient brother.
The cruel Pharaohs destroyed the mountains after you,
This lesson is enough for the world, my fortunate brother.
The enemies think your clothing looks like that of beggars,
You are inwardly a devotee, my efficient brother.
I have seen your calmness despite the restlessness,
This calmness is transferred to the friends of *Allah*, my brother.
You have not overcome the goals of immigration yet,
O, light-awaiting bright brother.

The tribe that you need for immigration,
Allah has made them the leaders, my honourable brother.
If you share the honour of immigration with me,
I will pray from my heart, my trench-fellow brother.

Jamal
July 17, 2008

London Life

There are clouds and rain but it doesn't have any character;
Life has little joy or happiness here.
Its bazaars and shops are full of goods,
These kinds of goods don't have a value.
Life here is so much lost in individuals that,
Brother to brother and father to son, there is no affection.
Here is a homeland of people that I can't talk about;
They get along with each other, but there is no love.
Don't expect happiness from life or being alive
When somebody doesn't have warmth in his heart.
These people are so caught up in life that
They don't find a single moment for simple human affection.
Their minds are fine, their bodies are fine and their technology is
    great,
But there is no stirring of love in their heart's blood.
This busy life, riding on the shoulders of technology,
Doesn't give them any joy these days either.
There are many parks with colourful flowers;
They don't have the freshness of the narcissus.
They walk around with ironed clean clothes and suits,
But they are not pure and clean on the inside.
Night and day they just think about whom they should fight;
They don't have any other skill.
Their knowledge is so great that they drill for oil in the depths of
    the oceans,
But even this knowledge doesn't give them a good reputation.
I see their many faults and virtues with my own eyes; but what
    can I say?
O Sa'eed, my heart doesn't have the patience to bear this.

Sa'eed
July 17, 2008

Ghazal

It cannot be built with two hands; we don't have four;
His brother has no hands to help the head of this ruined house;
Only wounded, damaged hopes are his support.
There are no other hands behind my wishes;
The rays of God's help have laid their hands on it;
There are no dark hands or dark clouds above it.
You offer a smile with your torn collar without pain;
The orphan said that these weren't his dear mother's hands;
There are many calamities that destroy things with help from the
    foreigners.
These are not the hands that would save their homeland from
    others;
They would choose bombs and artillery instead of change
As there are no great hands of our flowers.
O bountiful God! I am extending my hands of hope toward you;
My conscience tells me, Shirinzoy, that I have the right to true
    speech;
Allah is there; no matter if you don't have the hands of power.

Shahzada Shirinzoy
July 1, 2008

O God! These people!

O God! Change these people so that
Nobody will die by another's hand.
End cruelty so that
An ant won't die by someone's hand.
O God, for any thing to which you have given a soul
These things should never die by someone else's hand.
Reserve everyone's cruelty to their eyes
So no living thing will die by someone else's hand,
No traveller will be bitten by someone else's dog,
And nobody's dog will be killed by someone else's hand.

Mohammad Hanif Hairan
June 22, 2008

Star

The star which is stuck in black clouds –
Friends! That's my life's star.
It doesn't shine in the sky of my life;
Without light, it is seen clearly;
It walks asleep, separate from the caravan.
It fails to reach its destination, it is a joyless star;
Afghan conscience! Stop daydreaming!
No! Your star is the highest in the world,
Haidar! The opportunity for peace is not lost yet;
Your star is linked to danger.

Haidar
December 16, 2007

The Heart of Asia

O God! The world has hit me with stones for I am in love with
    you;
America hit me with stones in the name of terrorism.

My hands are tied; O God! I beg for victory;
From space the master of civilisation hits me with stones.

How fair is this? The world is astonished,
For the one I know hits me with stones and claims to be my
    friend.

The whole world is surprised because of my beauty,
That is the reason that the enemy hits the heart of Asia with
    stones.

Today, the world has really changed:
The grandson rises and pelts the grandfather with stones.

Oh Taif! I am angry and I complain to you:
Your son, on a bright day, hits my master with stones.

I beg of you O creator: destroy them like Abraha
The bastard Jewish generation hits my Aqsa[197] with stones.

They have joined the unbelievers and wish to destroy the
    Qur'an;
The Christians hit the *sunna*[198] of my pious prophet with stones.

I want you, O Nomial, to interpret this and tell me the truth:
The army of Islam is hitting the church with stones.

Nomial
December 11, 2006

This Oppressed Orphan Belongs to Which Martyr

This oppressed orphan belongs to which martyr?
Of which poor and oppressed martyrs is he?
The orphan, shaggy-haired with torn collar and wandering
He screams, he screams

You have remained far away from your companions and
    playmates
You have missed all the happiness of life
When the looks of his father vanished
All the stuff of life vanished from him
The rest of his life is enflamed, in pains, in fires
He screams, he screams

This oppressed orphan belongs to which martyr?
Of which poor and oppressed martyrs is he?
The orphan, shaggy-haired with torn collar and wandering
He screams, he screams

The orphan, who has been burnt in this censer,
Has been torched in the flames of loneliness
It seems like he has been torched in flames
His heart seems to have been pierced by arrows
He is a captive in the chains of oppression and cruelty
He screams, he screams

This oppressed orphan belongs to which martyr?
Of which poor and oppressed martyrs is he?
The orphan, shaggy-haired with torn collar and wandering
He screams, he screams

He screams and sighs
His collar, wet with tears
The funerals of wishes burn you
The lines of tears on his face burn him
He pretends to be eager and brave [...]
He screams, he screams

This oppressed orphan belongs to which martyr?
Of which poor and oppressed martyrs is he?
The orphan, shaggy-haired with torn collar and wandering
He screams, he screams

His pretty existence, when he passed away,
His beloved father with closed eyes
Says, "All my responsibilities have passed"
"All the happiness of my life has passed"
That is the reason Khwagman says that, "you are the instant of
    all regrets"
He screams, he screams

This oppressed orphan belongs to which martyr?
Of which poor and oppressed martyrs is he?
The orphan, shaggy-haired with torn collar and wandering
He screams, he screams

Khwagman
January 1, 2007

The young bride was killed here

I heard such bad news today that
Trembling came on my heart.

For the inhabitants of some village,
Today red flames rose up to the blue sky.
From the poetic atmosphere of that wedding,
My God, sounds like crying came.
Their pleasant songs were red with blood,
Roofs came down on every window.
The Pharaoh of the time was snoring there,
A flood of blood came here.
Black calamities wandered in the sky;

The black customs of grief came down to earth.
A mother is crying out of grief for her son,
Black evenings had arrived by morning.

I heard such bad news today that
Trembling reached my heart.

The young bride was killed here,
The groom and his wishes were martyred here.
The hearts full of hopes were looted here,
Not just those two but the whole group is martyred.
The children were murdered,
The story full of love is martyred here.
All their human rights were hurt,
The lover was martyred, the beloved is martyred.
The friends who were escorting them;
Alas, what beautiful youths are martyred.
The bride is drenched in red blood,
Her jewellery is broken and martyred.
Her hands are red with her blood;
Storms came upon her beautiful life.

I heard such bad news today that
Trembling reached my heart.

But the news brings press releases from Bagram,
Saying that "we have killed the terrorists."
How can we know the happiness of a wedding?
"We have killed many Afghans today.
This is a threat to our crusade,
That's why we killed those children."
They give the fighters' name to the bride,
They say that we only killed our enemies.
The president has appointed a commission once again:
"Go and see who they have killed."
Their pockets are filled not to say a word,
Because they have killed our relatives
As if the Red Forces came on their houses.

I heard such bad news today that
Trembling reached my heart.

For the inhabitants of some village,
Today red flames rose up to the blue sky.

August 18, 2008

The Burning Village

The burning village is being set alight,
 this village of pleasant wishes and desires.
Each brick is a piece of my heart,
 its clay is wet with the blood of the heart.
Its weather was good for the heart,
 this was the village where my spirit lived.

The burning village is being set alight

All my hopes lived there,
 all my desires bloomed there.
All my wishes would dance there,
 this is the village of all my concerns.

The burning village is being set alight

My youth's delight is hidden there,
 The echoes of its construction are hidden there.
My heart's restlessness is hidden there,
 this was the village of my merry desires.

The burning village is being set alight

All my emotions boiled over there,
 all my secrets were visible there.
All my grief would lighten there,
 this is the village of my grief and my happiness.

The burning village is being set alight

Each field of its farms marked the border of my grief,
 each part of its land is fallow for my songs.
Each of its bushes formed a nest for my wishes,
 this is the village of my grass and vegetables.

The burning village is being set alight

Life's desire hid in each yard,
 Hamon's madness hid in each house.
Today, tomorrow, yesterday: all are hiding in each of its rooms,
 this was the village of my hidden storms.

The burning village is being set alight

The struggle to rebel was alive everywhere,
 Other efforts were evident everywhere.
In everything, attempts to change were fiery,
 This was the village of my youthful concerns.

The burning village is being set alight

Words were like fire there,
 Intentions were harder than steel.
Contracts were pure profit,
 This was the village of hard-working tribes.
This village was built with my poems,
 With my nice quatrains and *ghazals*.
It was built with flowing floods,
 This is the village of my emotional artifice.

The burning village is being set alight

The enemies set fire to it,
 They made black smoke rise from its heart.
They turned its red rubies to soil and ashes,
 It has become a village of ruins.

The burning village is being set alight

Elham
October 28, 2008

Traveller Friend

You would not tell me that wailing is heard from your village;
You would not ask me why I am crying.
And

Why? Tears rolling down from your eyes?
You would not ask me what happened to the people in your
    village:
Those with moustaches
Those brave men
Those with turbans and long turban-ends
Those initiators of *jirga*
Those heroes of the Maiwand battles
Those strict Pashtuns
Those hospitable
Those sweet Pashtuns
Those who safeguarded Pashtu;
You would not ask me what happened to those muddy lanes;
You would not tell me why I am crying.
And
Why do I pour soil on my head[199];
You would not ask me what happened to those angel-girls:
The Pashtun girls,
Those dignified Pashtun girls,
The caravan of beautiful partridges on the ford;
Those strong female falcons of the Pamir;
Those pious daring women,
Those like Malalai and Nazo;
Those zealous women in the forts,
Screams of whose zeal would burst ear drums;
You would not ask me who ruined these houses.
You would not ask me why am I crying.
And
Who wounded me in the chest?
You would not ask me what happened to the small congregation:
The grey and dusty mosque,
The one in the middle of the village,
The pretty mosque without a door.
And
The tender Talib *Jan,*
The one with long hair,
The young Talib Jan,
Who used to cleanse hearts with his voice when he called the
    azan.
You would not ask me who these flags belong to and who these
    martyrs are.
You would not ask me why I am crying.
And

Whose are these orphans in tents?
Don't ask me, for God's sake!
I don't have to answer your questions;
This is the story of fate and misfortunes,
Of bombs, gunpowder, tales of death,
Stories of wailing and cries.
Don't ask me about it;
I can hardly dare tell them.
There are graves and cemeteries in every centimetre of earth,
    remaining for me
I don't know many martyrs and young-dead;
The crying from my lane is a flow of blood.
In my house and my village, the dragon has just given birth;
Water of the ford in my village is mixed with blood.[200]
Death has a contractor working in my village;
My villagers have been struck with a catastrophe.

Khalid Haidari
November 2, 2007

Laughing and Shouting

There is happiness, crying and complaints as well.
Our cheers and grief are mixed now, there is laughing and
    shouting.
In the morning they take the bride from the home and there is
    dancing and laughter,
In the evening there are screams and shouts in this village.
Some people are drenched in tears like an oil lamp,
With the fire on its head, it gives light and shouts.
This is the first word of the orphan child;
With his unsure tongue, he says "father, father."
Take something from this world with you and then return;
For the grave things of this world, shouting won't help.

Mohammad Qaseem Setoun
August 23, 2008

Spin Ghar

Villages are turned to ruins;
Their doors broken and scattered around in pieces.
Go to Spin Ghar and take a look;
Someone's hands, someone's legs can be found scattered there.
It seems that I don't love it anymore;
All the lanes are empty.
For those who played with the fate of our country,
There are only a few days left to take revenge.
As for me, Tala will cry for the grief of those
Whose funerals recently were held.

Tala Niyazi
December 16, 2007

Epic Cry

Mourning brought by cruelty and oppression; the entire world
   cries with me;
Complaints from relatives and strangers; the oppressed cry with
   me.
Our cottage was burned by the red dragon;
This poor and oppressed Afghan on a bad day cries with me.
Our sigh of pity rose higher than the sky;
Our collar, wet with warm tears, cries with me.
The places of our zeal and bravery were damaged;
The martyrs lying in the cemeteries cry with me.
Those who were crushed under the tank-treads without any
   guilt;
Children deprived of their fathers' shadows cry with me.
As their blood started to seep from their wounds,
From Sayyed Karam to Gyan, both cry with me.
Things happened in the cities instead of the deserts;
They cry with me in the middle of the city with their looted
   caravans.
Alive has disposed of life during its lifetime;
People were disabled; old and young cry with me.
Human dignity has been trampled, be careful;
The *Qur'an* – under piles of soil – cries with me.

These are the cries of Talayee and his incomplete wishes;
Poverty has became our zeal; the ruined homeland cries with me.

Abdul Kabir Talayee
May 27, 2008

Epic Ghazal

The enemy has come this day and wants a house in your village,
And wants to occupy each corner of our country.
They've come on purpose; young men be alert!
They've come to take revenge of the murders of Macnaghten
    and Brydon.
I guess there are other secrets behind the curtains;
The killer of the father wants to take the medal of Akbar Khan by
    force.
Like a sword, the handsome youths of my village were killed;
Still they want to slaughter some more with the knife.
They take lapis stones and my sword from the cradle of
    Badakhshan;
They want to leave a firm affront to our history.
This gun is the only memory of my martyred friend;
It costs but three dollars; they want someone's daughter.
If Akbar Khan and Ayyub Khan were to wake once more;
Such a youth requires a mother like Malalai.
Brothers of Latun! Think a little bit more!
Today the sisters of Malalai want our heads to be without caps.

Lutfullah Latun Tokhi
December 4, 2007

On *Eid*

When hearts die, the cheers die as well;
    Eid's day and Barat[201] nights are dead as well.
There is little sign of life in the graveyard;
    Other than that, our village's houses and alleys are dead as
    well.
We fear the warplanes' strikes;
    Barat's night's flames are put out.
The enemy fears the fire of joy;

The picnics of *Eid* are dead as well.
At your Christmas, Bagram is alit and bright;
On my *Eid*, even the rays of the sun are dead.
Suddenly at midnight, your bombs bring the light;
In our houses, even the oil lamps are turned off.
You set midnight aflame;
Our morning, our dawns are dead.
This is human love!? So strange! Why?
With every strike small girls die as well.
Blood and tears join with the waters;
That's why even our rivers don't ripple or surge.

Khepulwaak
December 7, 2008

Ghazal

We hear the noise of steel birds above our heads once again,
Over the houses of which poor people will they drop their
    bombs again?
The chief of the village claps for him with two hands;
They throw the flame of fire on our brides.
They never want such a life for their children;
They just throw heavy grief upon our happiness.
These people from around the world don't leave us be;
The time will come that the world will beg us.
The voice of *takbir* will break the heads of the arrogant;
My palaces will intone Malalai's poems.
He will never be in peace and allowed to rest,
He who throws the snow of his roof onto ours.

Sayyed Abdullah Nizami
August 3, 2008

Scream

Once again screams are heard from the top of the mountain over
    there;
Screams are heard from each valley, from each peak.
Again, a knife is put to the young body;
Painful screams are heard from the knife.

Did a shepherd die or was the young shepherd blown up by a
   bomb?
Over there, screams are heard from the head of cattle.
God! Who has been brought, beheaded by the river?
Girls cry, screams are heard from the bank of the river.
Someone is taken to Bagram and labelled "Al-Qaeda";
Screams are heard from the wings of the helicopter.
Leave us because you can't even control yourselves;
Even if you cry out a hundred times that you are a leader, O
   God!
The grief of Hejran will accompany him;
Screams are heard from the call of the *ghazal*.

Hejraan
December 4, 2007

The Burnt Veil

I came so tired to this village;
I said, the flames won't have reached here yet.
I thought I would forget the ashes and my burnt homeland;
That's why I came here with blisters on my feet.

How did you come here?
Were you troubled by life there as well?
No matter how much your collar was torn,
Why did you come through Boldak?

My God! Tell me, hasn't the sun risen there yet?
Your graveyards weren't full with the dead yet?
That smoke still hadn't spread around the village?
With veils on fire, weren't turbans too?

The veils are wet with the tears of separation;
My God, did they come for this reason?
Anger has been stirred;
Both revenge and complaints are brought by them.

Dost Mohammad Zondai
September 15, 2008

Our Village

There is a dead body with every step you take, my beloved,
Our tribe has been diminished by water, my beloved.
Their beautiful heads are not with their bodies,
The ropes are hanging at the gallows, my beloved.
My Kandahari sister is crying again today,
Somebody has killed her young brother.
There is red blood at every step,
A youth is just lying on it, my beloved.
This place from which two or three dead bodies are taken every
    hour,
This is our village, my beloved.
It's been a while that he moved away from the village,
Did you see the beloved, O Nu'man?

Mohammad Nu'man Dost
August 3, 2008

The Funeral of Desire

Nobody's funeral would be taken to the house of the
    disappointed,
With the funeral of one life taking the life of another.

This may be the cemetery of angels, it may enlighten a star,
but where will I hold the funeral of holy desire?

Come and grieve! To give one's shoulders for goodness,
So that, from the street on a whistle, the funeral melody is
    sounded.

Who would you find to moisten me with tears today?
To whom do you want to take my funeral in my empty village?

Like a pale face that vanishes by flying off,
Accept it as the funeral of meaning in the material universe.

What is life on earth? Merely we bury each other;
The funerals of everyone will take place on this earth.

O Spring! Who would be helpful for someone else in life?
Dawn carries the funeral of the night and the night of the dawn.

January 25, 2007

Ghazal

It's good that the palaces of the lords are tall;
We have a few cottages in their shadows.
Excuse me, God, what could be the reason for this?
There are wars and deaths only for Afghans.
Each mother of the homeland has been struck by the wind of
    grief;
All the mothers' sons have been killed here.
I count them good for refreshing the faith.
Who says bowing down to beauty must be contaminated by
    grief?
Our prayers have brought laden camels;
My holy God, the doors of your blessings are high.
But that martyr told his mother that he would come home soon;
How many nights has this poor mother spent waiting?
We are amazed, O God; we have lost our way.
Our shoulders are tired from bearing the coffins and our eyes
    from the tears.

Mohammad Hanif Hairan
June 22, 2008

On the Islands of Separation

On the islands of separation,
The watchman forgot the caravan.

In the storm of ignorance,
I forgot pain and remedy.

I am not aware of the situation anymore,
For tomorrow I think about today and yesterday.

Each chapter of my life
Is an exhibition of grief.

I hear someone moaning;
More and more I am not aware of what is happening.

I possess eyes and hands;
But, seeing and doing is not advised.

Why? These are no small feelings;
So what am I doing and what are the results?

I am not aware of good and evil
Because there I am choking on a sweet medicine.

I am asleep but my eyes open;
This is the mystery of such magic.

In abatement and stiffness, believe me!
One life is angry with the other.

For the happiness of strangers,
I have sacrificed my life and property.

And so at last, this is my situation,
Where the day of judgement is presented like a feast day.

Each chapter of my life
Is an exhibition of grief.

What should I do with the hands and feet given to me?
I cannot find life.

I am happy to be dumb rather than talkative,
It means I can't protest for my rights.

And I prefer to be blind,
When I can't observe dissimilation.

Such knowledge should be drenched in a flood;
I possess a mouth and I can't speak.

I have suffered and been set on fire many times;
My day and my night is surprised by attacks in the night.

Each chapter of my life
Is an exhibition of grief.

January 25, 2007

Complaint

There are no speeches of happiness here,
No speeches of brotherhood are being made.

I see everybody drenched wet with sweat;
Forlorn speeches are being made here.

Those who have money or power,
Give speeches of warmness.

There is a different world and law here,
Serious speeches are being given.

Nobody cares about one another here,
These are speeches of disappointment.

Your relatives look at you like strangers,
The speeches of relatives are less here?

When there was dedication and cordiality
Those former times and speeches are gone from here.

Walk on, O Afghan!
There are no speeches of the homeland being made here.

Afghani
August 23, 2008

Humanity

Everything has gone from the world,
The world has become empty again.
Human animal.
Humanity animality.
Everything has gone from the world,

I don't see anything now.
All that I see is
My imagination.

* *

Humanity is lost.
Afghaniyat is lost.[202]
Our zealous honour is lost as well.

* *

They don't accept us as humans,
They don't accept us as animals either.
And, as they would say,
Humans have two dimensions.
Humanity and animality,
We are out of both of them today.

* *

We are not animals,
I say this with certainty.
But,
Humanity has been forgotten by us,
And I don't know when it will come back.
May *Allah* give it to us,
And decorate us with this jewellery.
The jewellery of humanity,
For now it's only in our imagination.

Samiullah Khalid Sahak
August 22, 2008

In memory of the lost martyr

Your father seeks you in the mountains, your mother seeks you
    on the seas,
They stopped sleeping in your memory:
In which desert or valley do you lie?

Your father and mother keep your memory alive for ever;
Their graves are known in the graveyards;
There will always be many flags waving upon them.

For those who sacrifice their heads for the homeland,
The black soul will become gold with their blood;
The flowers take on the colour of the martyr's blood.

Uhud and Khandaq's mountains[203] are still red:
Many years have passed.
Who says the martyr's honour for the homeland is dead?

History writes his name in gold;
The tulip is coloured with your blood.
The heavens above take their colour from it as well.

Come and see what happened and what it is:
Blood streams innocently and becomes rivers;
The guesthouses of the Afghans are deserted.

Oh *Allah*! Bring back the old days!
Give trouble to the foreigner and whoever is cruel
So that they won't throw their heavy bombs upon us.

Oh *Allah*! Accept this prayer of mine!
Remove these pains and troubles of ours forever!
Sitting in the expectation of your mercy,
Khalilzai raises his hand toward you.

Khalilzai
November 28, 2008

Waiting for Freedom

I was burned in the caravan of darkness,
I was burned in the pain and grief of the country.
I wait for the freedom of my homeland.
For that I was burned in the flames of migration.
Nobody has expressed their condolences to me,
I was burned out of anxiety alone.
There is happiness all around the world;
I was always burned in the dark nights of grief.

Graveyard

To the west of this camp,
There is a beautiful graveyard.
At the top of a dusty hill,
There is the refugees' shrine.

Flags are hoisted up high,
Some are green and some are white.
Handkerchiefs are tied onto them,
They are so beautiful and colourful.

There is a silence in the graveyard.
There is no talk and no noise.
There is silence everywhere.
There are no gatherings and no speeches.

From time to time, groups of people
Come to the graveyard
And stand near the graves
And pray to *Allah*.

Then all of them go back
To their houses and residences.
Then for months and years
They don't look at the graveyard.

But amongst these graves
One of them can be seen from afar.
A martyr's tomb it is;
Its beauty is seen from the flags.

As I look at this grave,
Hope is buried there.
Warm wishes
Are buried there.

Every day when evening comes
And when the redness appears in the sky,
There is a mourning near this grave
And the sky just watches it.

A woman with a black veil
Comes to this grave
And sits near its tomb,
And then gradually starts crying.

What words of silent prayer
She speaks to herself.
She cries as if
unconscious.

And then she takes a nice handkerchief
And wraps it around the flag
And starts walking home.
She is even ready to give her life for him.

That's her whole life;
She lives in grief.
I don't know what's wrong with her,
But her youth is turning to soil.

As I see these incidents,
My heart splits into pieces.
With the situation of these poor widows,
My life becomes grief.

What cruelty is it that has brought
This grief to our nation.
Lights are snuffed on contact;
There is great grief and darkness.

Lutfullah
September 4, 2008

Glossary of Names and Terms

Ababeel
So-called green birds which attacked the advancing army of Abraha with pellets of hard-baked clay. See *sura* 105 for the Quranic account.

Abdali
This refers to the Durranis, one of the Pashtun tribes commonly found in southern Afghanistan.

Abraham
The Ethiopian Christian ruler of Yemen who – as referenced in *sura* 105, "the Elephant" – led a military expedition towards Mecca in 570.

Abraham
Abraham was a Prophet associated with the large monotheistic religions. He is cited in the *Qur'an* as such.

Abdul Ghaffar Bariyalai
Originally trained at the Dar ul-Ulum Deoband in India but later returned to Kandahar. He was well-known for his poems during the 1990s, and seems to have been regarded as a sort of spiritual and intellectual elder for the core of the original Talibs. He died in 2010.

Abu Bakr
(573–634). The father-in-law of the Prophet Mohammad. He was the first Caliph (following the death of Mohammad) and ruled from 632–634. He died of an illness in 634.

Jamaluddin al-Afghani
(1838–1897). A Muslim scholar and writer associated with the revivalist movement in Islamic thought.

Ahmad Shah Baba
(1722–1772). Born in Herat and a figure who went on to rule a huge empire stretching from India to eastern Persia. A Durrani Pashtun from Kandahar, he remains an important figure in the popular imagination.

Akbar Khan
(1816–1845). The Pashtun military and political leader famed

for his role in the battle of Gandamak in 1842. An area of
Kabul where many foreigners live is named after him.

Ali
The cousin and son-in-law of the Prophet Mohammad. He
ruled as Caliph from 656–661. He was the fourth of the
so-called *Rashidun* Caliphs that ruled after the death of the
Prophet Mohammad. Shi'a Muslims also regard Ali as the first
Imam. He was assassinated by a Kharijite in Kufa in 661.

Allahu Akbar
Arabic phrase literally translated as "God is the Greatest",
although more approximate to "God is Great".

Amanullah Khan
(1892–1960). Ruled Afghanistan from 1919–1929. He played
a prominent role in asserting the country's independence from
British interference and attempted to implement a reform
agenda. He moved too fast too soon, however, and was over-
thrown in an uprising. He abdicated in 1929 and went into
exile in India. He spent his remaining days in Europe (Italy
and Switzerland), dying in Zurich in 1960.

Amu
A large river that passes through northern Afghanistan. It is
also known as the Oxus river.

Atan
A traditional Pashtun dance. Participants move in a circle
while clapping their hands to the rhythm and spinning around.
One person leads the circle while the others follow his moves.
It is often performed at celebrations and weddings.

Ayyub Khan
(1857–1914). The ruler of Afghanistan from 1879–80. He
played a key role in the battle of Maiwand during the second
Anglo-Afghan war.

Azan
The *azan* is the Islamic "call to prayer", traditionally called
out by a *mu'azzin* from the top of a minaret, but nowa-
days often pre-recorded. It is the name of the recitation that
mosques broadcast to announce each of the five daily prayer
times. Also known as *adhan*.

Barat's Night
The so-called "night of deliverance" takes place on the four-
teenth day of the eighth month of the Islamic lunar calendar.

Dr William Brydon
(1811–1873). A doctor in the British Army during the first

Anglo-Afghan war. He was the only person to survive the retreat from Kabul via Jalalabad.

Bulbul

Pashto word for nightingale.

Dajjal

Means "impostor" and is an eschatalogical figure (akin to a sort of anti-Christ) in the Islamic tradition. The *dajjal* is not directly referenced in the *Qur'an* but is mentioned in the *hadith*s. The *dajjal* is reported to be blind in one eye in the *hadith* collection.

Farah

A province in the southwest of Afghanistan.

Farhad

One of the main characters in a Persian tragic romance, popularised in part by a telling by Nizami. The character of Farhad is sometimes referred to as Khosru. He was known to be extremely persistent, and to refer to someone's efforts as "Farhadi" is to remark that they are extremely committed.

Ghazal

A type of poem with its own rules for composition. It is one of the most common forms in the literature of the Middle East and South Asia.

Ghazi

Literally translates from the Arabic (but is used throughout the Muslim world) as "Islamic warrior" and is a loosely approximate alternative for the term *mujahed*.

Ghazni

A province in southern Afghanistan.

Boris Gromov, Gen.

(1943–). A Soviet soldier who was the last Russian to leave Afghanistan in February 1989. He is alive, and serves in the Russian State Duma.

Haidar

See Ali.

Mansour al-Hallaj

Condemned to death in 922 after expressing what were deemed to be heretical positions concerning man's relationship to God.

Hanafism

One of the four main Islamic schools of legal thought. It is predominant in Afghanistan (and is also one of the largest in terms of adherents globally). Named after the legal scholar

Abu Hanifa (d. 767), it advocates a more liberal approach to the Islamic law or *shari'a*.

Haram

A religious term used to denote that which is not permitted in Islam. It is the opposite of *halal* which literally translates as "that which is permitted."

Hatim al-Ta'i

(d. 578). A Christian poet from what we now call Saudi Arabia. His generosity was legendary even during his lifetime, and this reputation has continued among Arabs and the wider Muslim community.

Helmand

A province in southern Afghanistan.

Cave of Hera

Located in Saudi Arabia. It is a small opening in which the Prophet Mohammad first received his revelations that would become what we now know as the *Qur'an*. The first command made to him was *iqra*, or "recite".

Hijab

The head-covering cloth that some Muslim women choose to wear for religious reasons.

Hindu Kush

A mountain range that crosses Afghanistan and Pakistan.

Jamshid

(also known as Yima). A mythical King of Iran, about whom many stories have been written. His cup, the so called *Jaam-e Jaam*, was believed to have magical properties, allowing the user to foresee the future and/or to grant vast resources of power.

Jan

A Farsi/Dari term of endearment meaning "dear".

Jirga

A Pashto-language term meaning "council" or "consulta-tive gathering" It is to be distinguished from the word *shura*, although the two are sometimes used indistinguishably in a loose sense.

Joseph

Joseph (also known as Yusuf) is the slave taken into the house-hold of Potiphar whom Zuleikha seeks to seduce.

Kabul

A province of Afghanistan, and also the name of the country's capital city.

Kalima

This is the phrase all Muslims use to (re-)affirm their faith, and – if said three times in the presence of at least two witnesses – is also used when someone converts to Islam. Literally meaning "word" in Arabic, it is short for *kalimatu al-shahada*, or "the word (i.e. Phrase) of witnessing."

Kandahar

A province in southern Afghanistan.

Karbala

Karbala is a city in Iraq located southwest of Baghdad. A key battle between Hussein and forces loyal to the Umayyad Caliph Yazid took place there in 680 CE (in which Hussein was killed), and, as such it denotes an important moment in the history of Shi'ism.

Khalqi

Literally translated as "people" or "masses", the *Khalq* were a faction of the PDPA (People's Democratic Party of Afghanistan) headed by Noor Mohammad Taraki and Hafizullah Amin, and was opposed to the *Parcham* faction headed by Babrak Karmal.

Khan

A *khan* is a tribal chief and/or head of a community. Like *nawaab*, it is an honorific title often also used to describe those who own large portions of land. The title is usually placed after the name of a person.

Khotan

The editors believe this refers to the town and oasis located in Xinjiang Uyghur Autonomous Region of China, which historically hosted an Iranian-speaking population.

Khyber Pass

A mountainous passage linking Afghanistan to Pakistan.

Kuffar

Plural form of *kafir*. *Kafir* refers to a person believed to be in a state of *kufr* or "unbelief".

Kunar

A province in eastern Afghanistan.

Laghman

A province in the east of Afghanistan.

Laila and Majnun

The tragic love story of Leila and Majnun is a common reference in Afghan (and Persian) literature. It was first popularised by the Farsi-language poet Nizami.

Lowgar
A province south of Kabul.

William Hay Macnaghten
(1793–1841). Associated with the court of Shah Shuja. He attempted to support the Afghan King after the First Anglo-Afghan War but was killed when his divide-and-rule tactics were exposed.

Mahipar
A pass/crossing along the Hindu Kush through which people and goods are transported.

Mahmud Ghaznawi
(971–1030). A King who oversaw an empire out of Ghazni in what is now known as Afghanistan. His was a wealthy empire, and he sponsored many poets as part of his court.

Maiwand
A district in Kandahar province, also famous for being the site of a battle in 1860 during the second Anglo-Afghan war in which much of the British force was defeated.

Majnun
See Laila and Majnun.

Malalai
A woman who rallied Afghan fighters to return to the battle-field at Maiwand; she is remembered by Afghans of all political persuasions as a hero.

Malik
A localised version of a *khan*. The title is used to denote the local strongman on the district or sub-district level, and this often also means that person is somehow employed by the government to give some outreach for micro-management of particular issues.

Mangai
A kind of pot used as a water container.

Mihrab
The (often decorated or ornamental) recess set into the wall of a mosque to indicate the direction of Mecca for the purposes of prayer.

Minbar
A pulpit in a mosque from which the preacher or *Imam* delivers his sermons.

Mirwais Hotaki
A Pashtun ruler who oversaw a significant empire in present-day Afghanistan and Iran.

Mujahed

The active participle *mujahed* (plural *mujahedeen*) is a term used to refer to someone who is or was engaged in *jihad* (this almost always implies combat). It is used both as a noun ("a mujahed was killed") and adjectivally ("*haghe yaw mujahed saray wu*" in Pashtu; "he was a mujahed-type man"). The plural form is generally reserved for those Afghans who fought in the 1980s against their government and the Soviet army in Afghanistan. This usage is inherited and common among scholars.

Mullah

A religious functionary or cleric extremely prevalent outside the cities in Afghanistan. They will usually be the single religious authority (having attended a madrassa during childhood, or maybe because they can read some Arabic and thus the language of the *Qur'an*) in a particular village. As such, their authority is usually limited to religious matters.

Nangarhar

A province in the east of Afghanistan

Nazo

(1651–1717). A prominent female figure in Afghan history. She was a poet herself. Born in Kandahar, she was known as a courageous fighter as well. It is common for schools to be named after her.

Nimrod

A King (the great grandson of Noah) known both for building the tower of Babel, but also for a confrontation that he had with the Prophet Abraham. It is referenced in the *Qur'an*.

Omar ibn al-Khattab

(586–644). The second of the so-called *rashidun* Caliphs who ruled after the Prophet Mohammad's death. Omar succeeded Abu Bakr in 634 after the latter's death from an illness. He was a convert and a companion of the Prophet. He died in 644 at the hands of a Persian.

Osman bin 'Affan

(579–656). The third of the so-called *rashidun* Caliphs who took power following the death of the Prophet Mohammad. Osman succeeded Omar ibn al-Khattab and his rule oversaw a massive expansion of the territory under the control of the Caliphate. He was assassinated in 656.

Pahj

The soft silk-like cloth used for turbans; it often refers to the turban itself.

Paktika
A province in the southeast of Afghanistan
Palang
A large decorated/ornamental bed.
Pamir
The Pamir mountain range extends over Afghanistan, China,
Kyrgyzstan, Pakistan and Tajikistan.
Panjshir
A province to the north of Kabul.
Parcham
Literally translated as "flag", the *Parcham* were a faction of the
PDPA (People's Democratic Party of Afghanistan) headed by
Babrak Karmal, and was opposed to the *Khalq* faction led by
Noor Mohammad Taraki and Hafizullah Amin.
Patu
A *patu* is a woollen (or, nowadays, increasingly made from
synthetic materials) blanket worn by many Afghans as part
of their traditional dress. During the winter the material will
often be thick and woollen, whereas the summer variant of the
patu will be thinner. The *patu* is not just used to keep warm,
though; Afghans use it to sit on when outdoors, and often
perform their daily prayers on the very *patu* that they wear.
Pir Sayyed Ahmad Gailani
(1932–). The current head of the Qadiriyya Sufi order in
Afghanistan who led one of the groups officially sanctioned by
Pakistan to operate as jihadi fronts, the National Islamic Front
of Afghanistan. He used this spiritual authority along with
business clout and marriage into the Durrani Pashtun clan
to establish a large social hierarchy and organisation around
him. Still living in Kabul, he currently is as much politician as
he is religious leader. Yunus Qanuni is the former Speaker in
the Afghan parliament. He is from Panjshir province, served
together with Ahmad Shah Massoud during the 1980s and
1990s and currently heads a political party in Kabul.
Pizwan
A piece of jewellery hung from the nose, often worn by brides.
It is a pure Pashto word.
Pul-i Charkhi
A detention facility close to Kabul, which earned a particularly
bad reputation in the 1980s for the mistreatment of prisoners.
Night of Qadar
The night of *Qadar* or power is referred to in *sura* 97. It tells

of the night in which the revelation of the *Qur'an* was made to the Prophet Muhammad.

Qibla

An Arabic-language term that refers to the direction in which Muslims around the world pray (i.e. towards the *ka'aba* in Mecca (Saudi Arabia)). The *qibla* was originally oriented towards Jerusalem but this changed to the *ka'aba* in the year 623.

Qur'an

The holy *Qur'an* is the religious book of Muslims around the world, literally translated as "recitation" since Muslims believe it is the result of the direct revelation of God to the Prophet Muhammad starting in 610. The reference to "the best" may be found in *sura* 3, verse 110.

Rubab

An Afghan stringed musical instrument.

Sediq

See Abu Bakr.

Shah Shuja

(1616–1660) was the son of Mughal leader Shah Jahan;

Shamshad

A mountain (1544m high) in Nangarhar province.

Shari'a

This book follows Esposito's definition as "ideal Islamic law." There is a large body of thought which asks people to distinguish between *shari'a* and *fiqh* (human efforts to codify "Islamic" law in the absence of a specific injunction in the *Qur'an* or the *sunna*), arguing that the former is "ideal" and the latter is tainted and flawed. For this volume, the term *shari'a* is generally used to refer not only to the prescriptions and proscriptions themselves, but also the system surrounding it – the scholars and clerics whose role it is to interpret the law, as well as the *hadith* and *sunna* repository. There are five prominent schools of Islamic law: Hanafi, Hanbali, Maliki, Shafii and Ja'fari.

Sher Shah Suri

(1486–1545). A Pashtun who overthrew the Mughal empire in 1540, only to die accidentally from a gunpowder explosion in 1545.

Shi'a

Distinguished from the Sunnis, the *shi'i* are the so-called "partisans of Ali" (coming from the Arabic phrase *shi'at 'Ali*). Shi'i Muslims identify the fourth of the *rashidun* Caliphs, Ali, as the head of a line of leadership that they consider legitimate over the Sunni clerics that followed.

Shimla

This refers to the end of the turban hanging down. It denotes pride and dignity.

Spin Boldak

A district and town in Afghanistan. Located on the border with Pakistan, towards the south of Kandahar province.

Sunna

The established custom or precedent established and based on the example of the Prophet Muhammad. It offers a separate set of principles of conduct and traditions which were recorded by the Prophet's companions. These customs complement the divinely revealed message of the *Qur'an*. A whole field of jurisprudence has grown up alongside the study of the *sunna*. The *sunna* is recorded in the *ahadith* (plural of *hadith*). The *sunna* represents the prophetic "norm."

Takbir

"Allahu al-Akbar", a phrase often used as a chant or slogan.

Talib

Talib is the singular form of *Taliban*. *Alim* is the singular form of *Ulemaa'*. Literally "one who has knowledge", it refers to a religious scholar (primarily used for the Sunni clergy) who has been educated in the religious "sciences" (the *Qur'an*, the *sunna* and the *hadith*s etc).

Tarnak

A river in southern Afghanistan; it forms part of the Helmand river basin.

Tawhid

An Arabic-language term literally meaning "unity" and in an Islamic context refers to the belief that God is one/a single entity. It is a core principle of the Islamic faith.

Ulemaa'

Plural version of *'Alim*. Literally, "those who have knowledge", it refers to religious scholars (primarily used for *Sunni* clergy) who have been educated in the religious "sciences" (the *Qur'an*, the *Sunna* and the *hadith*s etc).

Umma

Umma is an Arabic-language term referring to the community of Muslims around the world. It is sometimes used in a secular form to mean "nation" (as in the Arabic version of "the United Nations," *al-Umam al-Muttahida*).

Uruzgan
A province in southern Afghanistan.

Wardak
A province west of Kabul.

Yazid
The Umayyad Caliph responsible for the death of Hussein.

Yima
See Jamshid.

Zabul
A province in southern Afghanistan.

Zakat
One of the five "pillars" of Islam; the practice of almsgiving is widespread and encouraged in southern Afghanistan. It is also – to a certain extent – systematised in such a way that it is in many instances a highly formalised type of charitable donation, whereby those with financial means must donate 2.5 per cent of their annual earnings and liquid assets for the needy. Apart from a nominal sum given to them by the government, the religious clergy – particularly in deeply rural areas of the south – often have to rely on *zakat* and other donations by their fellow villagers in order to survive.

Zuleikha
Potiphar's wife (as referred to in the *Qur'an* and the Bible).

Notes

1   "Interview With The Administrator Of The Islamic
    Emirate Website, Esteemed Brother Abdul Sattar
    Maiwand", http://theunjustmedia.com/Afghanistan/
    Statements/Feb11/Interview%20With%20The%20
    Administrator%20Of%20The%20Islamic%20Emirate%20
    Website,%20Esteemed%20Brother%20Abdul%20Sattar%20
    Maiwand.htm (accessed April 30, 2011).

2   http://www.afghanistan-today.org/article/?id=120
    (accessed January 24, 2012).

3   James Caron, "Reading the Power of Printed Orality
    in Afghanistan: Popular Pashto Literature as Historical
    Evidence and Public Intervention", *Journal of Social
    History*, vol. 45 no. 1 (2011), p. 184.

4   Thought to be tuberose flowers.

5   Benedicte Grima (2005), *The Performance of Emotion
    Among Pakhtun Women*. (Oxford: Oxford University
    Press).

6   See examples at http://www.magnumphotos.
    com/c.aspx?VP=XSpecific_MAG.BookDetail_
    VPage&pid=2K7O3R180KMO (accessed January 24,
    2012).

7   Note that we use the words poem, songs and *tarana* inter-
    changeably in this introductory essay, even though strictly
    speaking there are formal differences between them.

8   There are similar libraries of verse produced in Iraq and
    Somalia by forces opposed to external "invaders". See
    Jack Healy, "Sadrist Verse: Pen and Sword Meet in Poetry
    Contest," *New York Times*, June 9, 2011 for one such
    example.

9   In the words of one Talib interviewee: "Back then, when
    Rahman Baba was writing, it was all about love and
    philosophy. Different times emerged: it became about war
    and blood. The *tarana* are not really like the poems from
    Rahman Baba, but he set the scene."

10 The only exceptions were poems where we clearly identi-
    fied an author who was not a Talib, nor affiliated with the

movement; these were removed, as were poems by Rahman Baba and so on.

11 John Jeffcock (ed.) (2011), *Heroes: 100 Poems from the New Generation of War Poets* (Croydon: Ebury Press).

12 Both poets are also published occasionally on the Taliban's website.

13 This is, technically, the final line in the Pashto presentation of the poem; in translation the lines are split up into two for the most part.

14 D.N. MacKenzie (1958), "Pashto Verse", *Bulletin of the School of Oriental and African Studies*, vol. 21 1/3, pp. 319–33.

15 Caron (2011), 185.

16 Michael Semple, when asking a Talib about a recent military operation in southern Afghanistan, was given an MP3 track of a *tarana*; this was seen as all he needed to know. See Semple (2011), 1.

17 See Zaeef (2010), 43.

18 http://www.freemuse.org/sw34252.asp (accessed January 22, 2012).

19 Rosemary Moore (2000), *The Light in their Consciences: Early Quakers in Britain 1646–1666.* (Pennsylvania: Pennsylvania State University Press), 120–1; Pink Dandelion (2008), *The Quakers: A Very Short Introduction.* (Oxford: Oxford University Press), 13–4 and 23; Thomas D. Hamm (2003), *The Quakers in America.* (New York: Columbia University Press), 101–2.

20 Richard C. Martin (ed.) (2004), *Encyclopedia of Islam and the Muslim World.* (New York: Macmillan), 492–6; Lois Ibsen al-Faruqi (1985), "Music, Musicians and Muslim Law," *Asian Music*, vol. 17, No. 1 (Autumn-Winter), 3–36.

21 Alex Strick van Linschoten and Felix Kuehn (2012), *An Enemy We Created: The Myth of the Taliban/al-Qaeda Merger in Afghanistan, 1970–2010.* (London: Hurst).

22 John Baily (2009), "Music and Censorship in Afghanistan, 1973–2003" in Laudan Nooshin (ed.), *Music and the Play of Power in the Middle East, North Africa and Central Asia* (Farnham: Ashgate Publishing), 148.

23 Ibid., 152.

24 Ibid., 154.

25 Ibid., 153.

26 Ibid., 159.

27 Ibid., 157. See also: Suzanne Goldenberg, "Afghan trouba-dour now sings for Taliban," *Dawn*, November 17, 1998.

28 http://www.afghanistan-today.org/article/?id=120 (accessed January 24, 2012).

29 Baily (2009), 155–6; the *hadith* itself is taken from the collection of Ibn Hajar Haytami.

30 Rashid, 2001, 218–9

31 Manuscript copy, Kandahar.

32 Scott Johnson and Evan Thomas, "Mulla Omar Off The Record," *The New York Times*, January 20, 2002. http://www.thedailybeast.com/newsweek/2002/01/20/mulla-omar-off-the-record.print.html (accessed January 24, 2012).

33 Jon Lee Anderson (2003), *The Lion's Grave: Dispatches from Afghanistan*. (New York: Grove/Atlantic), 154–5.

34 Baily (2009), 160.

35 http://www.hrw.org/reports/2003/07/28/killing-you-very-easy-thing-us-0 (accessed January 24, 2012).

36 Dion Nissenbaum and Habib Khan Totakhil, "For Safety, Afghan Travelers Tune In to Taliban Ringtones," *Wall Street Journal*, December 28, 2011. http://online.wsj.com/article/SB10001424052970203733304577102093405583640.html (accessed January 24, 2012).

37 We were unable to locate an audio version. There were also some poems written by another female poet – Zarlasht Hafiz – published on the Taliban's website.

38 They are produced in Pakistan for the most part.

39 These were a small number compared to the rest of the collection. No more than two dozen poems were removed from the original complete sample.

40 There is, however, a long-standing tradition of women singing *tarana*, at least informally. One interviewee recalled a women baker singing such lyrics in the early 1980s about the Soviets.

41 Jere van Dyk (2011), *Captive: My Time as a Prisoner of the Taliban*. (New York: Macmillan), 167–8 and 191–2; David Rohde and Kristen Mulvihill (2010), *A Rope and a Prayer: A Kidnapping from Two Sides*. (New York: Penguin), 213 and 244.

42 "Ghazi" literally translates from the Arabic (but is used throughout the Muslim world) as "Islamic warrior" and is a loosely approximate alternative for the term "mujahed", albeit one with different cultural and historic connotations.

43 Note, too, that Guantánamo features heavily in Arabic-language jihadi poetry.

44 There were protests in May 2005 over the reported desecration of the *Qur'an* in Guantánamo, and again in April 2011. Guantánamo is mentioned dozens of times in the Taliban's statements that have been issued since the opening of the facility.

45 Joanna Nathan, "Reading the Taliban," in Antonio Giustozzi (ed.) (2009), *Decoding the New Taliban* (London: Hurst), p. 35.

46 Mark Falkoff (ed.), *Poems from Guantanamo: The Detainees Speak*, (Iowa City: University of Iowa Press, 2007)

47 Michael Semple breaks down the 71 poems he analysed in the following manner: 1 – elegies, 2 – "functional" propaganda, 3 – "pamphlets", 4 – "panegyrics", 5 – pastoral, 6 – satire. See Michael Semple, "Rhetoric of resistance in the Taliban's rebel ballads," Carr Center Paper for Harvard University, March 2011.

48 Jeffrey Brown and Daniel Sagalyn, "Poetry as a Weapon of War in Afghanistan," *PBS Newshour Art Beat*, March 25, 2011. http://www.pbs.org/newshour/art/blog/2011/03/taliban-poetry.html (accessed January 24, 2012). Note, too, that there is some precedent for foreign involvement in these cultural interactions; see Asadullah Shour (1988), *Oral Communications and their Historical Trajectory in Afghanistan* [in Dari]. (Kabul: Da Journalistano Ittihadia).

49 http://pinboard.in/u:strickvl/t:talibantwitterfight/ (accessed January 24, 2012).

50 Abdul Ghaffar Bariyalai was originally trained at the Dar ul-Ulum Deoband in India but he later returned to Kandahar. He was well-known for his poems during the 1990s, and seems to have been regarded as a sort of spiritual and intellectual elder for the core of the original Talibs. He died in 2010.

51 Jamshid (also known as Yima) was a mythical King of Iran, about whom many stories have been written. His cup, the so called *Jaam-e Jaam*, was believed to have magical properties, allowing the user to forsee the future and/or to grant vast resources of power.

52 The editors believe this refers to the town and oasis located in Xinjiang Uyghur Autonomous Region of China, which historically hosted an Iranian-speaking population.

53   Haidar is a reference to Ali (598–661) who was the cousin and son-in-law of the Prophet Mohammad. He ruled as Caliph from 656–661. He was the fourth of the so-called *Rashidun* Caliphs that ruled after the death of the Prophet Mohammad. Shi'a Muslims also regard Ali as the first *Imam*. He was assassinated by a Kharijite in Kufa in 661.

54   The tragic love story of Leila and Majnun is a common reference in Afghan (and Persian) literature. It was first popularised by the Farsi-language poet Nizami.

55   Shakib was the computer operator of Kandahar's Culture and Information Directorate during the Taliban's government in the 1990s.

56   The *azan* is the Islamic "call to prayer", traditionally called out by a *mu'azzin* from the top of a minaret, but nowadays often pre-recorded. It is the name of the recitation that mosques broadcast to announce each of the five daily prayer times. Also known as *adhan*.

57   This refers to a mosque.

58   A *patu* is a woollen (or, nowadays, increasingly made from synthetic materials) blanket worn by many Afghans as part of their traditional dress. During the winter the material will often be thick and woollen, whereas the summer variant of the *patu* will be thinner. The *patu* is not just used to keep warm, though; Afghans use it to sit on when outdoors, and often perform their daily prayers on the very *patu* that they wear.

59   Director of Kandahar's Literature Association during the 1990s.

60   Spin Boldak is located on the border with Pakistan, towards the south of Kandahar province.

61   This is a reference to the fourth caliph, Ali.

62   The Pamir mountain range extends over Afghanistan, China, Kyrgyzstan, Pakistan and Tajikistan.

63   "Jan" is a Farsi/Dari term of endearment meaning "dear".

64   Karbala is a city in Iraq located southwest of Baghdad. A key battle between Hussein and forces loyal to the Umayyad Caliph Yazid took place there in 680 CE (in which Hussein was killed), and, as such it denotes an important moment in the history of Shi'ism.

65   This seems to be a reference to al-Hajjaj ibn Yusuf, a governor of the eastern provinces of the Ummayad caliphate with a reputation for savagery.

66 There were total solar eclipses visible from Afghanistan on October 24, 1995 as well as August 11, 1999.

67 *Haram* is a religious term used to denote that which is not permitted in Islam. It is the opposite of *halal* which literally translates as "that which is permitted."

68 There are multiple hells in Islamic eschatology, each allocated for a separate category of individual.

69 Bulbul is the Pashto word for nightingale.

70 Shamshad is a mountain (1544m high) in Nangarhar province.

71 "Akbar's name" is a reference to *Allah*/God.

72 These are two rivers. The Amu is a large river that passes through northern Afghanistan. It is also known as the Oxus river. The Euphrates passes through Turkey, Syria and Iraq.

73 Maiwand is a district in Kandahar province, also famous for being the site of a battle in 1860 during the second Anglo-Afghan war in which much of the British force was defeated.

74 Malalai was a woman who rallied Afghan fighters to return to the battlefield at Maiwand; she is remembered by Afghans of all political persuasions as a hero.

75 *Batil* used here to refer to anything that isn't on the right/ Islamic path.

76 William Hay Macnaghten (1793–1841) was associated with the court of Shah Shuja. He attempted to support the Afghan King after the First Anglo-Afghan War but was killed when his divide-and-rule tactics were exposed.

77 Ibrahimkhil was an Urdu section officer during the Taliban's government.

78 Helmand is a province in southern Afghanistan.

79 Uruzgan and Kandahar are provinces in southern Afghanistan.

80 Zabul and Ghazni are provinces in southern Afghanistan.

81 Wardak and Lowgar are provinces near Kabul to the west and south.

82 Kunar is a province in eastern Afghanistan.

83 Paktika is a province in the southeast of Afghanistan, and Farah is a province in the southwest.

84 Nangarhar and Laghman are both provinces located in the east of Afghanistan.

85 The Hindu Kush is a mountain range that crosses Afghanistan and Pakistan. Mahipar is a pass/crossing along those

mountains through which people and goods are transported.

86   These are all mountains located in Afghanistan.

87   Plural version of *'Alim*. Literally, "those who have knowledge", it refers to religious scholars (primarily used for *Sunni* clergy) who have been educated in the religious "sciences" (the *Qur'an*, the *Sunna* and the *hadiths*, etc).

88   This refers to Ali, the fourth of the so-called *rashidun* Caliphs.

89   Omar ibn al-Khattab (586–644) was the second of the so-called *rashidun* caliphs who ruled after the Prophet Mohammad's death. Omar succeeded Abu Bakr in 634 after the latter's death from an illness. He was a convert and a companion of the Prophet. He died in 644 at the hands of a Persian attacker.

90   The Amu is a large river that passes through northern Afghanistan. It is also known as the Oxus river.

91   The Tarnak is a river in southern Afghanistan. It is part of the Helmand river basin.

92   This refers to the Helmand river, located in southern Afghanistan.

93   This refers to the Khyber Pass, a mountainous connective passage linking Afghanistan to Pakistan.

94   Panjshir is a province to the north of Kabul.

95   Kabul is a province of Afghanistan, and also the name of the country's capital city.

96   Abaceen is a common Pashto name, but also can mean "big sea".

97   The cave of Hera is located in Saudi Arabia. It is a small opening in which the Prophet Mohammad first received his revelations that would become what we now know as the *Qur'an*. The first command made to him was *iqra*, or "recite".

98   Zahid means ascetic in Arabic.

99   This is probably Abdul Shukur Rishad, a Pashtun nationalist historian who taught in the Oriental Institute in Leningrad in the early 1960s before returning to Afghanistan where he served a long career in the Kabul Pashto Academy. He died in recent years.

100   This refers to Mansour al-Hallaj who was condemned to death in 922 after expressing what were deemed to be heretical positions concerning man's relationship to God.

101   This refers to Abu Bakr, the first Caliph who ruled
      following the death of the Prophet Mohammad.
102   Plural form of *kafir*. *Kafir* refers to a person believed to be
      in a state of *kufr* or "unbelief".
103   This refers to Omar ibn al-Khattab, the second of the
      rashidun Caliphs.
104   Osman bin 'Affan (579–656) was the third of the so-called
      rashidun Caliphs who took power following the death of
      the Prophet Mohammad. Osman succeeded Omar ibn
      al-Khattab and his rule oversaw a massive expansion of the
      territory under the control of the Caliphate. He was assassi-
      nated in 656.
105   This refers to Ali ibn Abi Talib (598–661), the cousin and
      son-in-law of the Prophet Mohammad. He ruled as Caliph
      from 656–661. He was the fourth of the *rashidun* Caliphs
      that ruled after the death of the Prophet Mohammad. Shi'a
      Muslims also regard Ali as the first Imam. He was assassi-
      nated by a Kharijite in Kufa in 661.
106   This literally translates as "the one, the one".
107   Bilal ibn Rabah was an Ethiopian former slave chosen by
      the Prophet Mohammad to proclaim the first Muslim call
      to prayer in the year 630.
108   This is an expression meaning that someone attempts to
      make the situation so bad that nobody can benefit from it.
109   This refers to Hatim al-Ta'i (d. 578), a Christian poet
      from what we now call Saudi Arabia. His generosity was
      legendary even during his lifetime, and this reputation has
      continued among Arabs and the wider Muslim community.
110   *A'jam* refers to non-Arabs.
111   The holy *Qur'an* is the religious book of Muslims around
      the world, literally translated as "recitation" since Muslims
      believe it is the result of the direct revelation of God to the
      Prophet Muhammad starting in 610. The reference to "the
      best" may be found in *sura* 3, verse 110.
112   *Umma* is an Arabic-language term referring to the commu-
      nity of Muslims around the world. It is sometimes used in a
      secular form to mean "nation" (as in the Arabic version of
      "the United Nations," *al-Umam al-Muttahida*).
113   The *mihrab* is the (often decorated or ornamental) recess
      set into the wall of a mosque to indicate the direction of
      Mecca for the purposes of prayer.
114   Pious Muslims wear a cap during prayer (and often during
      the rest of the day as well).

115 The night of *Qadar* or power is referred to in *sura* 97. It tells of the night in which the revelation of the *Qur'an* was made to the Prophet Muhammad.

116 Talib is the singular form of Taliban. *Alim* is the singular form of *Ulemaa'*. Literally "one who has knowledge", it refers to a religious scholar (primarily used for the Sunni clergy) who has been educated in the religious "sciences" (the *Qur'an*, the *sunna* and the *hadiths*, etc).

117 Zuleikha is Potiphar's wife (as referred to in the *Qur'an* and the Bible).

118 Joseph is the slave taken into the household of Potiphar whom Zuleikha seeks to seduce.

119 Nimrod was a King (the great grandson of Noah) known both for building the tower of Babel, but also for a confrontation that he had with the Prophet Abraham. It is referenced in the *Qur'an*.

120 Abraham was a Prophet associated with the large monotheistic religions. He is cited in the *Qur'an* as such.

121 This refers to Isaac.

122 This is a kind of poem, the authors of which are unknown.

123 *Tanha* literally translates as "alone".

124 The red and white in this line refer to gold and silver.

125 Gul Pacha Olfat was a privately-trained *alim* from a small landowning *sayyid* family of Nangarhar. He was head of the Kabul Pashto Academy in the 1950s, and was editor of several prominent periodicals. He died just before the Saur coup.

126 This refers to the Umayyad Caliph responsible for the death of Hussein.

127 Panipat refers to a battle in a small town in what we now term India.

128 Ghilzai and Mohmad are both names of Pashtun tribes.

129 A *mangai* is a kind of pot used as a water container.,

130 The *pizwan* is a piece of jewellery hung from the nose, often worn by brides. It is a pure Pashto word.

131 This refers to Omar ibn al-Khattab, the second Caliph following the death of the Prophet Mohammad. He was given the title *al-Faruq* on the basis of his ability to distinguish between right and wrong.

132 Farhad refers to one of the main characters in a Persian tragic romance, popularised in part by a telling by Nizami. The character of Farhad is sometimes referred to as Khosru. He was known to be extremely persistent, and to

235

refer to someone's efforts as "Farhadi" is to remark that they are extremely committed.

133 This refers to two great poets of the Pashto literary canon, Rahman Baba and Khushal Khan Khattak.

134 A *ghazal* is a type of poem with its own rules for composition. It is one of the most common forms in the literature of the Middle East and South Asia.

135 This refers to the head-covering cloth that some Muslim women choose to wear for religious reasons.

136 Note on the title: *dajjal* means impostor and is an eschatalogical figure (akin to a sort of anti-Christ) in the Islamic tradition. The *dajjal* is not directly referenced in the *Qur'an* but is mentioned in the *hadiths*.

137 The *dajjal* is reported to be blind in one eye in the *hadith* collection.

138 This is a reference to the US detention facility at Guantánamo Bay.

139 Nazo (1651–1717) was a prominent female figure in Afghan history. She was a poet herself. Born in Kandahar, she was known as a courageous fighter as well. It is common for schools to be named after her.

140 The green mark is a small tattoo or mark that some women in Afghanistan put on their foreheads. It is a common trope for poets to refer to these marks.

141 This refers to Amanullah Khan (1892–1960) who ruled Afghanistan from 1919–1929). He played a prominent role in asserting the country's independence from British interference and attempted to implement a reform agenda. He moved too fast too soon, however, and was met with uprisings in response. He abdicated in 1929 and went into exile in India. He spent his remaining days in Europe (Italy and Switzerland), dying in Zurich in 1960.

142 This refers to Akbar Khan (1816–1845), the Pashtun military and political leader famed for his role in the battle of Gandamak in 1842. An area of Kabul where many foreigners live is named after him.

143 This refers to Mahmud Ghaznawi (971–1030) a King who oversaw an empire out of Ghazni in what is now known as Afghanistan. His was a wealthy empire, and he sponsored many poets as part of his court.

144 Hanafism is one of the four main Islamic schools of legal thought. It is predominant in Afghanistan (and is also one of the largest in terms of adherents globally). Named after

the legal scholar Abu Hanifa (d. 767), it advocates a more liberal approach to the Islamic law or *shari'a*.

145 The *saqi*, in a tradition that dates back to classical Arabic poetry, is the wine-bearer.

146 It is unclear exactly which Pir the poet is referring to in this line, but the implication is that there are a large number of shrines in the space where people are meant to be living.

147 A *ghazi* literally translates from the Arabic (but is used throughout the Muslim world) as "Islamic warrior" and is a loosely approximate alternative for the term *mujahed*.

148 The rubab is an Afghan stringed musical instrument.

149 A *mullah* is a religious functionary or cleric extremely prevalent outside the cities in Afghanistan. They will usually be the single religious authority (having attended a madrassa during childhood, or maybe because they can read some Arabic and thus the language of the *Qur'an*) in a particular village. As such, their authority is usually limited to religious matters.

150 This refers to the army of Yazid, the Umayyad Caliph who was responsible for the death of Hussein.

151 Note that the Pashto words for pot and water spring both are romantic references (because it would usually be women who would bring the pots with water from the springs).

152 The *atan* is a traditional Pashtun dance. Participants move in a circle while clapping their hands to the rhythm and spinning around. One person leads the circle while the others follow his moves. It is often performed at celebrations and weddings.

153 The Spin Ghar mountain range extends from Afghanistan into Pakistan over some 100 miles.

154 This is referring to Ahmad Shah Baba (1722–1772), born in Herat and a figure who went on to rule a huge empire stretching from India to eastern Persia. A Durrani Pashtun from Kandahar, he remains an important figure in the popular imagination.

155 This refers to Ayyub Khan (1857–1914), the ruler of Afghanistan from 1879–80. He played a key role in the battle of Maiwand during the second Anglo-Afghan war.

156 The active participle *mujahed* (plural *mujahedeen*) is a term used to refer to someone who is or was engaged in *jihad* (this almost always implies combat). It is used both as a noun ("a mujahed was killed") and adjectivally ("*baghe*

yaw mujahed saray wu" in Pashtu; "he was a mujahed-type man"). The plural form is generally reserved for reference to those Afghans who fought in the 1980s against their government and the Soviet soldiers inside Afghanistan. This usage is inherited and common among scholars.

157   For *shari'a* this book follows Esposito's definition as "ideal Islamic law." There is a large body of thought which asks people to distinguish between *shari'a* and *fiqh* (human efforts to codify "Islamic" law in the absence of a specific injunction in the *Qur'an* or the *sunna*), arguing that the former is "ideal" and the latter is tainted and flawed. For this book, the term *shari'a* is generally used to refer not only to the prescriptions and proscriptions themselves, but also the system surrounding it – the scholars and clerics whose role it is to interpret the law, as well as the *hadith* and *sunna* repository. There are five prominent schools of Islamic law: Hanafi, Hanbali, Maliki, Shafii and Ja'fari.

158   An interesting parallel may be found in the Baluch poem "I am a rebel" by Gul Khan Naseer, which repeats similar themes and also the repeated refrain. See Arif (2010), 86–7.

159   This is a reference to Mirwais Hotaki, a Pashtun ruler who oversaw a significant empire in present-day Afghanistan and Iran.

160   *Qibla* is an Arabic-language term that refers to the direction in which Muslims around the world pray (i.e. towards the *ka'aba* in Mecca (Saudi Arabia)). The *qibla* was originally oriented towards Jerusalem but this changed to the *ka'aba* in the year 623.

161   This refers to Sher Shah Suri (1486–1545), a Pashtun who overthrew the Mughal empire in 1540, only to die accidentally from a gunpowder explosion in 1545.

162   This literally translates from Pashto as "black mountain".

163   This literally translates from Pashto as "white mountain".

164   Moustaches naturally droop downwards at the edges of the mouth, but some people fold their moustache hairs upwards to signify bravery as Genghis Khan was known to do.

165   The *pahj* is actually just the soft silk-like cloth used for turbans, but in reality it often refers to the turban itself.

166   *Jirga* is a Pashto-language term meaning "council" or "consultative gathering" It is to be distinguished from the word *shura*, although the two are sometimes used indistinguishably in a loose sense.

167 A large decorated bed.

168 *Zakat* is one of the five "pillars" of Islam; the practice of almsgiving is widespread and encouraged in southern Afghanistan. It is also – to a certain extent – systematised in such a way that it is in many instances a highly formalised type of charitable donation, whereby those with financial means must donate 2.5 per cent of their annual earnings and liquid assets for the needy. Apart from a nominal sum given to them by the government, the religious clergy – particularly in deeply rural areas of the south – often have to rely on *zakat* and other donations by their fellow villagers in order to survive.

169 This is referring to Genghis Khan, who led the Mongol conquests in the thirteenth century.

170 Literally translated as "flag", the *Parcham* were a faction of the PDPA (People's Democratic Party of Afghanistan) headed by Babrak Karmal, and was opposed to the *Khalq* faction led by Noor Mohammad Taraki and Hafizullah Amin.

171 This refers to the Durranis, one of the Pashtun tribes commonly found in southern Afghanistan.

172 A *minbar* is a pulpit in a mosque from which the preacher or *Imam* delivers his sermons.

173 There were 41 countries in the ISAF coalition when the poem was written. There are currently (as of February 2012) 50 countries contributing troops to ISAF.

174 Muntazir Zaidi is the Iraqi journalist who threw his shoe at President George W. Bush in December 2008.

175 This refers to Laura Bush, the wife of US former President George W. Bush; and Condoleezza Rice, the former US Secretary of State (under George W. Bush).

176 Pir Sayyed Ahmad Gailani (1932–) is the current head of the Qadiriyya Sufi order in Afghanistan and led one of the groups officially sanctioned by Pakistan to operate as jihadi fronts, the National Islamic Front of Afghanistan. He used this spiritual authority along with business clout and marriage into the Durrani Pashtun clan to establish a large social hierarchy and organisation around him. Still living in Kabul, he currently is as much politician as he is religious leader. Yunus Qanuni is the former Speaker in the Afghan parliament. He is from Panjshir province, served together with Ahmad Shah Massoud during the 1980s and 1990s and currently heads a political party in Kabul.

177 Shah Shuja (1616–1660) was the son of Mughal leader Shah Jahan; Babrak Karmal was the President of Afghanistan, installed by the Soviets at the time of the military invasion in 1979; Hamid Karzai is the current serving President of Afghanistan.

178 This is a reference to different Pashtun tribes.

179 Arabic phrase literally translated as "God is the Greatest", although more approximate to "God is Great".

180 This refers to Somnath, the site of the temple in India destroyed by Mahmud Ghaznawi.

181 This refers to Dr. William Brydon (1811–1873), a doctor in the British Army during the first Anglo-Afghan war. He was the only person to survive the retreat from Kabul via Jalalabad.

182 This refers to Boris Gromov (1943–), a Soviet military figure who was the last to leave Afghanistan in February 1989. He is alive, and serves in the Russian State Duma.

183 These are all ethnic groups found in Afghanistan.

184 This refers to Jamaluddin al-Afghani (1838–1897), a Muslim scholar and writer associated with the revivalist movement in Islamic thought.

185 Literally translated as "people" or "masses", the *Khalq* were a faction of the PDPA (People's Democratic Party of Afghanistan) headed by Noor Mohammad Taraki and Hafizullah Amin, and was opposed to the *Parcham* faction headed by Babrak Karmal.

186 Distinguished from the Sunnis, the *shi'i* are the so-called "partisans of Ali" (coming from the Arabic phrase *shi'at 'Ali*). Shi'i Muslims identify the fourth of the *rashidun* Caliphs, Ali, as the head of a line of leadership that they consider legitimate over the Sunni clerics that followed.

187 "Allahu al-Akbar", a phrase often used as a chant or slogan.

188 This refers to the end of the turban hanging down. It denotes pride and dignity.

189 Abraha was the Ethiopian Christian ruler of Yemen who – as referenced in *sura* 105, "the Elephant" – led a military expedition towards Mecca in 570.

190 This refers to the *ababeel* or so-called green birds which attacked the advancing army of Abraha with pellets of hard-baked clay. See *sura* 105 for the Quranic account.

191 This is the phrase all Muslims use to (re-)affirm their faith, and – if said three times in the presence of at least two witnesses – is also used when someone converts to Islam.

Literally meaning "word" in Arabic, it is short for *kalimatu al-shahada*, or "the word (i.e. Phrase) of witnessing."

192 A *khan* is a tribal chief and/or head of a community. Like *nawaab*, it is an honorific title often also used to describe those who own large portions of land. The title is usually placed after the name of a person.

193 Note, that in the imagery of Pashto poetry, the nightingale to the lawn is comparable to the citizen to their homeland.

194 *Tawhid* is an Arabic-language term literally meaning "unity" and in an Islamic context refers to the belief that God is one/a single entity. It is a core principle of the Islamic faith.

195 This refers to a detention facility close to Kabul, which earned a particularly bad reputation in the 1980s for the mistreatment of prisoners.

196 A *malik* is a localised version of a *khan*. The title is used to denote the local strongman on the district or sub-district level, and this often also means that person is somehow employed by the government to give some outreach for micro-management of particular issues.

197 This refers to the Al-Aqsa Mosque in Jerusalem.

198 The established custom or precedent established and based on the example of the Prophet Muhammad. It offers a separate set of principles of conduct and traditions which were recorded by the Prophet's companions. These customs complement the divinely revealed message of the *Qur'an*. A whole field of jurisprudence has grown up alongside the study of the *sunna*. The *sunna* is recorded in the *ahadith* (plural of *hadith*). The *sunna* represents the prophetic "norm."

199 This is an expression signifying exasperation or regret that something has taken place.

200 The Pashto original refers to an amount of water that could be contained in the cup of both hands.

201 Barat's night, or the so-called "night of deliverance" takes place on the fourteenth day of the eighth month of the Islamic lunar calendar.

202 Afghaniyat can be loosely translated as "Afghan-ness".

203 This refers to two battles fought during the time of the Prophet Mohammad. The battle of Uhud was fought in 625, and Khandaq, or the trench, was fought in 627.

Select Bibliography

Ahmad, Aisha and Roger Boase (2003), *Pashtun Tales from the Pakistan-Afghan frontier*. (London: Saqi Books).

Anderson, Jon Lee (2003), *The Lion's Grave: Dispatches from Afghanistan*. (New York: Grove/Atlantic).

Arif, Iftikhar (2010), *Modern Poetry of Pakistan*. (Champaign: Dalkey Archive Press).

Atal, Naqib Ahmad (2011), "Underground anthems of war," *Afghanistan Today*, June 20. http://www.afghanistan-today. org/article/?id=120 (accessed 2 February 2012).

Baily, John (2001), "Can You Stop the Birds Singing? The Censorship of Music in Afghanistan," *Freemuse*, April, http:// www.freemuse.org/sw1106.asp (accessed 2 February 2012).

Baily, John (2009), "Music and Censorship in Afghanistan, 1973–2003" in Laudan Nooshin (ed.), *Music and the Play of Power in the Middle East, North Africa and Central Asia* (Farnham: Ashgate Publishing).

— (2010), "The Censorship of Music in Afghanistan," *RAWA*, 26 July, http://www. rawa.org/music.htm (accessed 18 January 2011).

Baldick, Julian (1975), *Mystical Islam: An Introduction to Sufism*. (Chapel Hill: University of North Carolina Press).

Bartlotti, Leonard, Mohammad Nawaz Tair and Raj Wali Shah Khattak (2006), *Rohi Mataluna: Pashto Proverbs*. (Peshawar: Interlit Foundation and Pashto Academy).

Caroe, Olaf (1964), *The Pathans*. (London: Macmillan).

Caron, James (2011), "Reading the Power of Printed Orality in Afghanistan: Popular Pashto Literature as Historical Evidence and Public Intervention", *Journal of Social History*, vol. 45 no. 1.

Case, Dean J. and Robert Pawlak (2010), "Winning the Battle of Narratives in Afghanistan" in JSOU, Essays JSOU Report 10/4. (Florida: Joint Special Operations University).

Coghlan, Tom (2005), "Writing poetry was the balm that kept Guantanamo prisoners from going mad," *San Francisco Chronicle*, July 17. http://www.sfgate.com/cgi-bin/

article.cgi?f=/c/a/2005/07/17/MNGKQDPCV51. DTL&type=printable (accessed 2 February 2012).

Darmesteter, James (1888/1974), *Chants Populaires des Afghans*. (Amsterdam: Philo Press).

David, Alfred and James Simpson (eds) (2006), *The Norton Anthology of English Literature: Volume A, The Middle Ages*. (New York: W.W. Norton).

Dupree, Louis (1978), *Afghanistan*. (Princeton: Princeton University Press).

Dyk, Jere van (2011), *Captive: My Time as a Prisoner of the Taliban*. (New York: Macmillan).

Edwards, David (1993), "Words in the Balance: The poetics of political dissent in Afghanistan," in *Russia's Muslim Frontiers* (ed.) Dale Eickelman (Bloomington: Indiana University Press), 114–129.

— (1993), "Summoning Muslims : print, politics and religious ideology in Afghanistan," *Journal of Asian Studies*, vol. 52 no. 3, 609 628.

Emadi, Hafizullah (2005), *Culture and Customs of Afghanistan*. (Westport: Greenwood Press).

Falkoff, Marc (ed.) (2007), *Poems from Guantánamo: The Detainees Speak*. (Iowa City: University of Iowa Press).

al-Faruqi, Lois Ibsen (1985), "Music, Musicians and Muslim Law," *Asian Music*, vol. 17, no. 1 (Autumn-Winter), 3–36.

Ferlinghetti, Lawrence (1975), *Poetry as Insurgent Art*. (New York: New Directions Books).

Foxley, Tim (2007), *The Taliban's propaganda activities: how well is the Afghan insurgency communicating and what is it saying?* (Stockholm: SIPRI). http://www.sipri.org/research/conflict/publications/foxley (accessed 2 February 2012).

Freemuse (2007), "Taliban Group Issues New Ban on Sale of Music", 23 August, http://www.freemuse.org/sw21167.asp (accessed 2 February 2012).

Gall, Carlotta (2008), "Afghans Want a Deal on Foreign Troops," *The New York Times*, 25 August. http://www.nytimes.com/2008/08/26/world/asia/26afghan.html (accessed 18 January 2011).

Goldenberg, Suzanne (1998), "Afghan troubadour now sings for Taliban," *Dawn*, November 17.

Grima, Benedicte (2005), *The Performance of Emotion Among Pakhtun Women*. (Oxford: Oxford University Press).

Harsent, David (2005), *Legion*. (London: Faber & Faber).

Healy, Jack (2011), "Sadrist Verse: Pen and Sword Meet in Poetry Contest," *New York Times*, June 9. http://atwar.blogs. nytimes.com/2011/06/09/sadrist-verse-poetry-contest-cele-bratesiraqi-resistance/ (accessed 2 February 2012).

Human Rights Watch (2003), *Killing You is a Very Easy Thing For Us: Human Rights Abuses in Southeast Afghanistan.* (New York: Human Rights Watch). http://www.hrw.org/reports/2003/07/28/killing-you-very-easy-thing-us-0 (accessed 2 February 2012).

Hussain, Raja G. (2008). *The Impact of Collateral Damage on the Taliban Insurgency.* (Monterey: Naval Postgraduate School). http://www.au.af.mil/info-ops/iosphere/08fall/iosphere_fall08_hussain.pdf (accessed 2 February 2012).

Jamal, Mahmood (ed.) (2009), *Islamic Mystical Poetry.* (London: Penguin).

Jeffcock, John (ed.) (2011), *Heroes: 100 Poems from the New Generation of War Poets.* (London: Ebury Press).

Johnson, Scott and Evan Thomas (2002), "Mullah Omar Off The Record," *New York Times*, January 20. http://www. thedailybeast.com/newsweek/2002/01/20/mulla-omar-off-the-record.print.html (accessed January 24, 2012).

Johnson, Thomas (2007), "The Taliban Insurgency and an Analysis of Shabnamah (Night Letters)," *Small Wars and Insurgencies*, vol. 18, no. 3, September, 317–44.

— (2010), "Religious Figures, Insurgency, and Jihad in Southern Afghanistan," in *Who Speaks for Islam? Muslim Grassroots Leaders and Popular Preachers in South Asia*, NBR Special Report #22 (Seattle: The National Bureau of Asian Research), February, 41–65.

Johnson, Thomas and Ahmad Waheed (2011), "Analyzing Taliban taranas (chants): an effective Afghan propaganda arte-fact," *Small Wars and Insurgencies*, vol. 22, 3 31.

Loewen, Arley and Josette McMichael (2010), *Images of Afghanistan: Exploring Afghan Culture through Art and Literature.* (Oxford: Oxford University Press).

MacKenzie, D. N. (1958), "Pashto Verse," *Bulletin of the School of Oriental and African Studies*, vol. 21, no. 1/3, 319 333.

Martin, Richard C. (ed.) (2004), *Encyclopedia of Islam and the Muslim World.* (New York: Macmillan).

Motlagh, Jason (2009), "Why the Taliban is winning the Propaganda War," *Time*, April 5. http://www.time.com/time/printout/0,8816,1895496,00.html (accessed 2 February 2012).

Nathan, Joanna (2008), *Taliban Propaganda: Winning the War of Words?* (New York: International Crisis Group).

— (2009), "Reading the Taliban," in Antonio Giustozzi, *Decoding the New Taliban: Insights from the Afghan Field.* (London: Hurst).

Nissen, Thomas Elkjer (2007), *The Taliban's Information Warfare.* (Copenhagen: Royal Danish Defence College). http://ics.leeds.ac.uk/papers/pmt/exhibits/2919/The_Talibans_information_warfare.pdf (accessed 2 February 2012).

Nissenbaum, Dion and Habib Khan Totakhil (2011), "For Safety, Afghan Travelers Tune In to Taliban Ringtones," *Wall Street Journal*, December 28. http://online.wsj.com/article/SB10001424052970203733304577102093405583640.html (accessed January 24, 2012).

Rohde, David and Kristen Mulvihill (2010), *A Rope and a Prayer: A Kidnapping from Two Sides.* (New York: Penguin).

Roy, Oliver (1990), *Islam and Resistance in Afghanistan.* (Cambridge: Cambridge University Press).

Rzehak, Lutz (2011), *Doing Pashto: Pashtunwali as the ideal of honourable behaviour and tribal life among the Pashtuns.* (Kabul: Afghanistan Analysts Network). http://aan-afghanistan.com/index.asp?id=1567 (accessed 2 February 2012).

Saed, Zohra and Sahar Muradi (2010), *One Story, Thirty Stories: an anthology of contemporary Afghan American literature.* (Fayetteville: University of Arkansas Press).

Sakata, Hiromi (1983), *Music in the Mind: The Concepts of Music and Musician in Afghanistan.* (Kent: Kent State University Press).

Salahuddin, Sayed (2010), "Karzai Orders Probe into Afghan Civilian Deaths Reports," *Reuters*, 5 August. http://www.reuters.com/article/idUSTRE6741KP20100805 (accessed 2 February 2012).

Samatar, Said (1982), *Oral Poetry and Somali Nationalism.* (Cambridge: Cambridge University Press).

Schimmel, Annemarie (1975), *Mystical Dimensions of Islam.* (Chapel Hill: University of North Carolina Press).

Schmeck, Dereck I. (2009), *Taliban information strategy: How are the Taliban directing their information strategy towards the population of Afghanistan?* (Monterey: Naval Postgraduate School). http://edocs.nps.edu/npspubs/scholarly/theses/2009/Dec/09Dec_Schmeck.pdf (accessed 2 February 2012).

Semple, Michael (2011), "Rhetoric of resistance in the Taliban's rebel ballads," Carr Center Paper for Harvard University, March. http://www.hks.harvard.edu/cchrp/research/working_papers/Semple_RhetoricOfResistanceInTheTalibanTuranas.pdf (accessed 2 February 2012).

Shinwari, Abdul Wakil Sulamal (2009), *Fifty Million Short Stories*. (Pittsburgh: Dorrance Publishing).

Shour, Asadullah (1988), *Oral Communications and their Historical Trajectory in Afghanistan* [in Dari]. (Kabul: Da Journalistano Ittihadia).

Siddique, Abubakar (2009), "British Ethnomusicologist: 'It Isn't Actually Correct To Say Taliban Have Banned Music'," *Radio Free Europe / Radio Liberty*, June 22. http://www.rferl.org/articleprintview/1753865.html (accessed 2 February 2012).

— (2010), "Freedom of Musical Expression, Understanding the Taliban's Campaign against Music," *Freemuse*, July, http://www.freemuse.org/sw34252.asp (accessed 18 January 2011).

Straziuso, Jason (2009), "The Kabul Quagmire," *Associated Press*, 17 October. http://freerepublic.com/focus/f-news/2364626/posts (accessed 2 February 2012).

Trimingham, Spencer (1971), *The Sufi Orders of Islam*. (Oxford: Clarendon Press).

Yousafzai, Khushal (2010), "Freedom of Musical Expression: Music has Died in the Swat Valley," *Freemuse*, 15 July. http://www.freemuse.org/sw33496.asp (accessed 2 February 2012).

Zaeef, Abdul Salam (2010), *My Life With the Taliban*. (London: Hurst).